"Witty, relevant, and offers wonderful encouragement to those of us in the depths of the mothering trenches...A breath of fresh air for moms everywhere."

—**Mary Byers,** speaker and author of *The Mother Load: How to Meet Your Own Needs While Caring for Your Family*

"Cindy proves you are never too old to fall in love with mothering all over again. Practical, spiritually uplifting, and hilarious, this book is one I'll be recommending to all my friends."

—**Heidi Bratton,** mother of five, columnist, and author of *Making Peace with Motherhood...and Creating a Better You*

"With flat-out honesty and humor, Cindy covers everything from the transition to stay-at-home status, to tips to keep your sex life with hubby sizzling, to how to start a book club, to streamlining the whole getting-a-meal-on-the-table process. You will immediately be able to put these wonderful ideas into practice."

—**Lisa Espinoza Johnson,** author of *Days of Whine and Noses—Pep Talks for Tuckered-Out Moms*

"For any mother who has ever cried in the night because being a mom is the most difficult job in the world—this book will lift your spirits, give you hope, and make you smile."

—**Debbie Lamb,** mother of three, pastor's wife, part-time professor at Dallas Christian College

Who Got PEANUT BUTTER on My Daily Planner?

Cindy Sigler Dagnan

HARVEST HOUSE PUBLISHERS

EUGENE, OREGON

Cover by Terry Dugan Design, Minneapolis, Minnesota

Cover illustration © Terry Dugan Design

Back-cover author photo © Vintage Tyme Photograph

Cindy Sigler Dagnan is published in association with the literary agency of WordServe Literary Group, Ltd., 10152 S. Knoll Circle, Highlands Ranch, CO 80130.

WHO GOT PEANUT BUTTER ON MY DAILY PLANNER?
Copyright © 2006 by Cindy Sigler Dagnan
Published by Harvest House Publishers
Eugene, Oregon 97402
www.harvesthousepublishers.com

Library of Congress Cataloging-in-Publication Data
Dagnan, Cindy Sigler, 1965-
    Who got peanut butter on my daily planner? / Cindy Sigler Dagnan.
    p. cm.
    ISBN-13: 978-0-7369-1824-4 (pbk.)
    ISBN-10: 0-7369-1824-8 (pbk.)
    Product # 6918244
    1. Stay-at-home mothers—Religious life.   2. Christian women—Religious life.   3. Dagnan, Cindy
Sigler, 1965- I. Title.
    BV4529.18.D36 2006
    248.8'431—dc22   2006001339

Printed in the United States of America

06 07 08 09 10 11 12 13 14 / BP-MS / 10 9 8 7 6 5 4 3 2 1

For my own four sweet blessings, Eden, Emmy, Ellie, and Elexa, who make it possible for me to carry around my own peanut-butter-smeared planner. I treasure every moment.

For my mother, Patsy Sigler, who embodies everything the word mother *should mean.*

For my husband and hero, Greg Dagnan, who inspires me to be better every day.

Acknowledgments

Greg Johnson, my incredible agent—every time I write, I am thankful God sent you and precious Becky as an answer to prayer.

LaRae and Carolyn—you made me fall in love with Harvest House from our first conversation! Thanks for letting me play too.

Hope Lyda—you are an angel wearing an editor's hat. I laugh my abs into better shape reading your e-mails. I know we must be like souls.

The cover designers and the sales and marketing team at Harvest House—wow! When I get to meet you in person, I shall come bearing chocolate.

Anna Macklin and the Thursday afternoon Bible study group—thanks for saying, "So why don't you just quit whining about your deadline and write already?"

Sharris, Vickie, Patsy, Kathryn—thanks for reading the roughest of drafts.

Stephanie Reagor—thanks for letting everyone see your kryptonite hang out!

Tom and Ginny—thanks for desks, cubbies, awesome food, and surprise visits. Your friendship is a great perk of Christian fellowship.

Sharris Paris, Victoria Jo, KarenKay, Pattycake, Lins—exactly how much fun should one book club have? Who needs to fear 40? Ocean breezes, shark bait, Hi! Lucy—"can't wait!" I love you all. It was the best worst trip I've ever been on.

Mother—thanks for being my biggest fan. Daddy—I sure hope you can see this from heaven; I still remember...Annie—I never thought I'd grow up to love my "baby" sister so much. You've come a long way from when you dropped our dolls on the floor and dragged them around by their hair. Your skill as a mother amazes me.

My four girls—you will always be my babies. When being a mommy was at the top of my list of things I wanted to be when I grew up, I never knew it could be this wonderful.

Greg—you have seen our planner, not just matted with peanut butter, but with missing pages, crayon scribbles, and crumpled edges. That you love me anyway humbles me. Thanks for being so much fun to try all the new material with!

To all the moms I meet while speaking—you inspire me to keep my writing in the real world.

Father God—I stand in awe. You have taken the desires of my heart and made them not just grow, but flourish. May every word be Your own.

Contents

How to Really
Have It All

*You may outgrow almost
everything else in your life,
but never your childhood.*

—Source unknown

The alarm went off at 5:56 AM. I groaned and fumbled for the snooze button as I ticked off a list of the day's chores in my mind. Scrambled brains, not scrambled eggs, would be on the menu for this breakfast. *Load briefcase, graded papers, backpack, coloring books, bottle bag, and diaper bag into vehicle. Drop children at sitter's. Spout off a rapid list of directions to sitter while simultaneously writing a check for one child's book-club order and wiping the other's baby vomit off my right shoulder. Swing by for prescription at drive-up pharmacy. Teach three classes. Pick up dry cleaning and buy cookies for school party on my planning period. Scarf down Snickers and Diet Coke for lunch. Teach three more classes. Take oldest child to ballet. Grade papers while waiting. Come home, start dinner, read four story books, finish dinner, vacuum, eat dinner, do dishes, give kids a bath, feed puppy, hear prayers, rock baby, pat husband on head and tenderly whisper,*

9

"*Maybe tomorrow night, dearest.*" *Fall asleep lamenting the lack of time to do anything remotely resembling devotions.*

And then I got out of bed.

One kindergartner and one sleepy six-month-old had to be out the door and in the van with me by seven A M. Only someone who has had a kindergartner could appreciate the hopelessness of my task. Surely, next to the dictionary entry for *dawdle* is a picture of my oldest daughter.

I was growing very weary of "having it all." And I had it all, that's for sure. The dark under-eye circles. The sound of my voice bellowing, "Hurry up, we'll be late!" echoed in my ears as I arrived at the high school looking decidedly like a *Glamour don't.* I wiped away the tears that emerged the moment I dropped the kids off at the sitter's house. My oldest looked like she'd grown up too fast, and the baby looked tender and vulnerable in that priceless, just-awakened way.

And on this morning I knew something had to give. The thoughts and questions began. *What if I didn't do this anymore? What if I just stayed home?*

So began the first of several months of praying, questioning, vacillating, discussing, and researching the possibility of quitting work and staying home. My husband was very supportive; we began actively looking for ways to make this new dream a reality.

I purchased and read Larry Burkett's practical book *Women Leaving the Workplace.* While his budget predictions sometimes seemed a bit idealistic, they inspired me and my husband to make this list of all expenses related to my work:

+ a large wardrobe
+ dry-cleaning services
+ child care
+ meals out or snack-machine allowances
+ gasoline

- miles and maintenance on a second car
- supplies, bulletin-board materials, and extra resources for my classroom
- stock in Tylenol for tension headaches
- nagging feelings of guilt and inadequacy
- placement in a higher tax bracket
- feelings of short-changing either my family or my students
- less sleep

The bottom line was that it *cost* us for me to be at work.

On the flip side, I loved teaching. I thrived on the challenge of inspiring high school juniors and seniors to care about history, government, and sociology. I empathized with their heartbreaks and rejoiced over great dates, knock-out prom pictures, and newly acquired scholarships. I liked preparing my advanced-placement students for college. I enjoyed knowing I could influence them for good and make a difference in their lives.

I also had a newly completed master's degree. Wouldn't I be wasting all that education? What would happen to my seven years of teaching? Hadn't I always considered the public high school a personal mission field? Would I miss the adult companionship? The thrill of those lightbulb moments when a student truly grasped a difficult concept? The golden moments when a student, by letter or return visit, thanked me for being their teacher, for giving them something they could use? The e-mails from college, updating me on their lives and accomplishments?

But growing ever stronger was the conviction I would still be a teacher at home and the realization that impacting the lives of classroom students wouldn't mean anything if I lost the chance to influence the children I loved more than life itself. (And happily, people are always producing more children for me to teach later.)

The clincher was recognizing this truth: Even if I could afford to pay someone to do all the tasks I do, I could not pay them enough to love, spend time with, nurture, or share my values with my children.

So the process began. I read books about staying home. I worked overtime, teaching a night class, with the baby in a playpen and the oldest at the chalkboard, earning money to reduce our debt. I scouted out part-time or work-at-home possibilities. I explored any option that would allow me more flexibility and more time with my family.

I asked my oldest daughter, Eden, about her feelings. Did she want me to be at home? Did she understand that in the realm of the "Kingdom of Things," it would mean less for her? What would she like best about me being at home? What would she like least?

I talked with other women whom I respected and admired. Of those who stayed home, I asked, "Why did you do it?" and more urgently, "*How* are you doing it?" One mother, a bank manager, shared this with me as we stood together at a school party. "I love my job. It has so many benefits. They even pay me to volunteer two hours a week at my son's school. I'm just so stressed all the time, I'm not sure it's worth it anymore." I knew that feeling all too well.

⎯

I have been home with my four little girls, either full- or part-time now, for seven years. I treasure what Eden told her daddy one day last fall: "My favorite time of day is when I get off the school bus and Mommy is standing there on the porch waving and waiting for me. I know when we get inside, there'll be snacks and she'll listen all about my day."

One of the most difficult aspects of making the transition from working full-time to staying at home was the reaction to my announcement. My colleagues were mystified and full of questions: *Why are you leaving? You're so good at your job! I thought you loved teaching! What will you do all day?* My students were incredulous: *Mrs. D, you can't do this! I thought you liked us! Can't you wait until our senior year?* Our families were support-ive but concerned: *Have you done the math on this? Are you sure you can make it?* After they were assured that this had been a prayerfully consid-ered decision, they backed us 100 percent and reminded us God would provide. And He has, sometimes in remarkably unexpected ways.

More and more evidence is being gathered that supports active paren-tal involvement in our children's lives. Current magazine covers list articles about the value of volunteering in schools, being there for homework time, setting boundaries, and lavishly dispensing hugs. Last fall I read a report that sharing several family dinners together each week is one of the top indicators of high SAT scores. Kids whose parents take an active part in their education get better grades and into less trouble in school. Chil-dren whose parents are physically affectionate and who model compas-sion tend to turn out the same way.

I think we mothers have known this for a long time. Society is just now catching up to us. Remember the criticism Princess Diana got for taking her babies along on royal visits? Remember the contrast between the news photos of Diana running, arms outstretched, to meet her boys after a separation—and the regal but chilly Queen Elizabeth, who greeted a young Prince Charles with a mere handshake?

If you've come to the place where you desperately want to be there more for your children, pray about it and take the plunge. If you've already jumped into the water of being at home, keep treading—because the thrills of high-dive days and the fun of back-float days will be more than you can imagine.

Chapter 1

The House That Stress Built

The ordinary acts we practice every day
at home are of more importance to
the soul than their simplicity might suggest.

—*Thomas Moore*

All of us want to be there for our children—we just don't want to lose ourselves in the process. One of the most difficult aspects of staying home is the loneliness and isolation. Any woman can easily be launched into pity-party territory when she faces never-ending laundry and dishes and very little adult interaction. Michelle, a mother of three in Indiana, wrote, "It's very easy to get tired and then start feeling sorry for yourself. 'Poor me, stuck here at home.' Everyone else's life looks more glamorous. Don't fall into that trap—our job is most important!"

Shelly, a mother in Texas, told me, "It is very difficult to have adult relationships. My husband gets tired of hearing about homemaking only. My friends are either working or too busy with more children than I have. I sometimes feel like a boring person."

We are afraid of losing our own identities. We secretly wonder, *I love being a mother, but is that all I'm ever going to be—someone's mom?* A young mother of a two-year-old boy said, "I often forget who I am!"

Nancy, a mother of four, echoes this feeling: "I am a different person than I used to be. I change as quickly as the children—I can hardly keep up to know who I am." There is no getting around the fact that our lives are not the same after children.

But what can we do about our isolation? How can we truly love our days at home? It is my goal to encourage you, inspire you, give you some practical tools to organize your days, provide you with some jumping-off points for your own wonderful creativity, and to love you through these pages.

Getting Started

Allow me to give you an overview of some things we'll journey through in this book:

Be productive. Choose to do things for others. Volunteer selectively. Send notes of encouragement. When baking for your family, make extra for a neighbor, shut-in, or friend. Read a book. Learn a new skill. Make time for exercise. Make a point of getting dressed, really dressed, first thing in the morning. For many women, the way we feel and our productivity are tied to the way we look. Give yourself that boost.

One of the biggest potential time-wasters for every homemaker is the television. Have it off much more than you have it on. Mothers tell me about two struggles on this front. One group struggles because they leave the television on all day just for the background noise of adult voices. My heart goes out to them. When my husband was on the three-to-midnight shift at work, I had huge chunks of the evening to myself after the children were in bed, and I struggled with waves of loneliness. I craved the low hum of voices and the psychedelic blink of the screen too.

Yet another group struggles because they adore soap operas. One mom actually requested prayer; she really wanted to break what she felt was a wasteful, and possibly negative, habit. I shared with her how

I broke my former habit (purely by accident). One day, I had the television volume turned way up so I could hear my favorite show (okay, it was *Santa Barbara*) while I was off in the kitchen trying to finish the dishes during a commercial break. I happened to hear the last few minutes of the previous soap opera before mine was scheduled to begin. But, I couldn't *see* the players.

Why is this significant, you ask? Because without scenes, costumes, and actors, the poorly scripted dialogue is flat, the voices melodramatic, and the plotlines lame. *Doorbell rings in background.* I imagine a ridiculously well-dressed woman (supposedly a stay-at-home mom) or a maid in formal uniform gliding to the door. A male voice anguishes, *"Oh, Angelina, are you still pregnant? How can this be? I thought that when you rode with my cousin and accidentally witnessed that mob killing you miscarried!"* Loud, heart-wrenching sobs break out—I assume from Angelina. *"Oh, Trenton* (or some other impossibly soap opera-ish name), *I didn't think you'd* (dramatic sniff, hiccup) *find out—it's not our baby. It never was— it's..."* At that point I was laughing so hard at the utter ridiculousness of what I was hearing that I snorted my Coca-Cola up my nose—and that awful burning sensation broke me of my habit forever!

While television does offer some great stuff, the bulk of it is shallow. It breeds dissatisfaction with your own life by making you compare your body/house/meals/love life to that of unrealistic, impossibly beautiful, over-made-up people who can afford haircuts every two weeks. Many of the talk shows are depressing and degrading, if not downright immoral. Don't let the television babysit your children either. Offer alternatives: Simon Says, books, marbles, puzzles, colors, play dough and cookie cutters. Most of the television watching in our house is done with the VCR and DVD players; that way we choose the programs.

Get out of the house. I used to meet girlfriends twice a week at our local mall to walk. We arrived before the stores opened to avoid the crowds and the temptation to shop. With our children tucked in strollers and baby joggers, we walked laps, visited, laughed, and de-stressed. Aside from the health benefits (well, since we sometimes snacked and often got so involved in our conversation that our strides turned to shuffles, those might be minimal), the adult conversation and the contact with others who are experiencing similar circumstances is awesome. One of our walking crew was a brand-new mom who hadn't gotten off the couch or out of her jammies until we dragged her out. She told us she couldn't believe the difference in her outlook when she had the walks to look forward to. If you're experiencing a housebound week, invite a friend over to talk while your kids play together.

Establish and maintain female friendships. It is both unfair and unrealistic to expect our husbands to meet every need we have. Develop healthy interests and friendships of your own. I have talked to so many women who want nothing more than to get out of the house after having been stuck there all day. Their husbands long for nothing more than a quiet evening at home, remote control in hand. Rather than discuss the problem and arrive at a mutual solution with their husbands, they all brood in hurt silence. Rescue both of you from this no-win situation by renewing old friendships and seeking out new ones. Try these ideas:

+ Join a women's Bible study or MOPS group that offers on-site child care.
+ Make plans with some buddies for an annual get-away at one of the Hearts at Home conferences.
+ Join a book club or create your own.
+ Sign up for an evening craft class at a local hobby store or enroll in a college extension class.
+ Strike up conversations with other mothers at the store, at church, at school. Chances are they're feeling isolated too.

+ Go to one of those fun six to midnight scrapbooking and stamping fests.

+ Make the first move. Invite a few friends to go to a movie or to come over to your house for an evening of pedicures, popcorn, movie candy, and chick flicks!

+ Plan activities for yourself and your children. Start a play group.

+ Take your children to story time at the local library.

+ Take the children to visit the fire station, a local museum, a bakery, the police department.

+ Go with another mom and her kids to the zoo or local swimming pool.

+ If your husband works a night shift or frequently travels, go to the airport field at night and watch the lights as the planes land. These miniature field trips educate the kids, liberate you, and go a long way toward beating cabin fever.

Cultivate a hearty sense of humor. The truth is, kids, and our lives with them, are hilarious. Get a fun-patterned spiral notebook and start jotting down the cute things they say or do, together with the date and their age. Whenever possible, tuck a snapshot of the moment in next to it. Not only will it be fun to look back on, but it will craft a touching and priceless log of your days together.

Two of my recent entries describe funny names that Ellie, four, and Elexa, two, have given to common objects. One day Ellie wanted a piece of paper for coloring. But what she asked was, "Mommy, can I please have a piece of your printing complete paper?" I couldn't think what she wanted, so I asked her to just show me. She led me to the stack of plain white sheets stacked in my computer's printer. Whenever it's done printing, the computer announces, "Printing complete." So, that's how she thought of it!

My just-turned-two-year-old got to go on her first roller-coaster ride in the kid's section of Silver Dollar City. We called it the baby coaster, and she had a ball. The next night when we got home, I asked the girls to get coasters out of the basket for their drinks. Elexa looked very confused. "Not a coaster. A baby coaster. I ride. Was fun. Scary." She giggled. Her big sisters patiently explained that those were also coasters. "I need a baby coaster for my 'nink' too," she announced.

"There is only one thing about which I shall have no regrets when my life ends. I have savored to the full all the small, daily joys. The bright sunshine on the breakfast table; the smell of the air at dusk; the sound of the clock ticking; the light rains that start gently after midnight; the hour when the family comes home; Sunday evening tea before the fire! I have never missed one moment of beauty, not ever taken it for granted. Spring, summer, autumn or winter. I wish I had failed as little in other ways."

Agnes Sligh Turnbull

Pray about it. The old hymn is beautifully true and comforting: "Oh, what peace we often forfeit; oh, what needless pain we bear. All because we do not carry everything to God in prayer." Tell God what you need and how you feel. Remember that you are made in God's image and are exactly where He wants you to be. There is no emotion we have that He has not experienced. Yes, that includes feeling unappreciated and abandoned!

Depression often sets in when we are too introspective. When that happens, pray for others. Get the focus off of yourself. Make it a habit to cut out the prayer list from the church paper or bulletin. Tape it on your car dash, refrigerator, or mirror and pray for those needs. Let your children see you pray. Pray for them. Encourage them to pray for others, and teach them how to pray for themselves when they are hurt, lonely, thankful, or scared.

Focus. Motherhood is an important job. You may not do it perfectly, but you do it best. If you forget this truth, don't worry—your kids will remind you. One incident stands out in my mind. I was busy preparing to speak to some fellow teachers at a training seminar. Eden was pestering me, pulling at me for attention. Exasperated, I said shortly, "Eden, all Mommy really wants to do is finish this work!" She turned away and in a tiny voice replied, "All you really want to do is play with me." Naturally I dropped everything for a cuddle and then patiently installed her next to me at the table with a marker and transparency of her own.

Remember, this is just a season of life, ever-changing, flying by. Life is too short for regrets. Too fleeting for feeling guilty. Too marvelous to be too busy.

Together, let's discover how to leave behind the house that stress built. It is possible when you...

- gain tools for making your at-home days more efficient, productive, and meaningful.
- learn practical shortcuts for maximizing the hours in your day.
- discover that perfectionism is a load you can drop and that caring for yourself as well as your family is essential.
- gather and use some streamlined and yummy information on meal planning.
- apply some new organizational strategies.
- practice some fun tips for making your home a hospitable one.
- leaf through ideas to springboard creativity for shaping a

comfortable home that reflects your family and provides a retreat from the stress of the world.

Throughout this book, at the end of each chapter will be scripture verses, journaling ideas, an action plan, and study and reflection questions you may use alone or for group study. It is my fervent prayer that this book will transcend the dailiness of our responsibilities and bring us closer to the One who invented the marvelous concept of home!

———

Sure, you've traded job stress for a different kind of stress, but life is infinitely sweeter in many ways. I pray that this journey we share will guide you to organize and love your days as a mom. I want to encourage you, pray for you, and motivate you. You are many things. You occupy many roles. But your place as wife and mother is one only you can fill. Plan for it. Pray about it. But most of all, laugh along on the journey.

QUESTIONS FOR STUDY AND REFLECTION

1. If you'd like to, share about the circumstances surrounding your decision to stay at home. What do you love about it? What is the hardest thing for you?

2. What one area mentioned in this chapter are you hoping most to improve?

3. Read Psalm 101:3 and Philippians 4:8. Are these principles and admonitions true of the television viewing and reading material in your home? What helps you set standards?

4. Read Matthew 6:23-32 and then rewrite it in the space below, including your name and some of the specific things you want and are concerned about, as though it were a personal promise to you... because it is!

5. One of my favorite verses in the Old Testament is Psalm 5:3. Read through it this week, and try voicing your praises first, and then your requests, even as you are fumbling for the alarm clock and rubbing the sleep from your eyes. Throughout the day, plan to "wait in expectation" and be alert for all the ways in which God is helping give you strength, grace, and unexpected blessings. Read Jeremiah 29:11 and fill in these blanks:

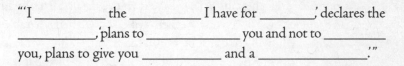

   "'I _____ the _____ I have for _____,' declares the _____, 'plans to _____ you and not to _____ you, plans to give you _____ and a _____.'"

   How does the truth of this promise impact your role as a homemaker?

6. Make a list of all the things that are causing you stress in your life. Rank them in order from largest to smallest stressor. Now put all of them through the "Big Deal Scale" test. Will this thing matter to me in five years? In one year? Next week? Tomorrow? If not, turn it over to God and make a concerted effort to leave it with Him. If it helps you, cut a narrow slit in a small box (you type A's out there can cover it with contact paper, wrapping paper, or decoupage). During your prayer time, write down what is worrying you or causing you stress, pray over it, and place it in your box. Later it will be a great boost to look back on how you've grown in worry control

and perhaps jot down how God has answered a request, fulfilled a longing, or quenched a worry.

7. Go back and read the Agnes Turnbull quote (see page 20). Have you been "savoring to the full" the small daily things? If not, what is keeping you from that?

Action Plan

Look through magazines for a beautiful photograph from nature, one which reflects the current season. Cut it out in the shape of a heart or in a beautiful square, edged with decorative scissors. On a smaller piece of cut-to-fit plain paper, write or type these five beautiful words from Scripture: "He himself is our peace" (Ephesians 2:14). Tape it to the dashboard of your car, the window above your kitchen sink, or your bedside table—anywhere you will look and be reminded that the One who made the stars has your home, indeed your very life, in His capable hands.

Journal

Purchase yourself a beautifully bound journal. You will be using it for several things throughout this book. Make your first entry a dream blueprint for your home. Cut pictures of the styles and décor you love most. Jot down ideas for traditions. Write what you love about being home and the kind of atmosphere you'd like to create there.

Memorize

"Unless the LORD builds the house, its builders labor in vain" (Psalm 127:1).

Chapter 2

Kryptonite and
the Supermom

*Children never put off till tomorrow
what will keep them from
going to bed tonight.*

—*Evan Esar*

All moms, at one time or another, have faced the realization—*This is not what I thought it would be; this is not how I thought I would be.* And of course such thoughts are swallowed with a chaser of guilt. I haven't met a mother who hasn't occasionally been shocked by the disparity between expectations and reality.

We hold tightly to a dream version of our life because we love fairy tales and we love superheroes. I selected my first pair of eye glasses with Superwoman in mind. I just knew that if I wore them, I could leave my sixth-grade desk, spin around—and my long hair would tumble down gracefully, and bullet-deflecting bands of gold would magically appear on my wrists. And back then my thighs would have looked great in that royal blue, yellow, and red suit with white stars! I was sad when the superhero line of Underoos came out—I was too old to wear them.

The Supermom syndrome begins with the tiny seed of a dream and gives birth way before we do. It can be traced to the first moment we chuck the birth-control pills, prop pillows under our hips, and become maniacal about our cycles. Or perhaps it starts the day we scrape our life savings together, scrounge pennies from sidewalks and the change from underneath the couch cushions, apply for a loan, take a deep breath, and apply at the adoption agency.

It doesn't matter how you get there—you just do. You dream of a little girl to dress in pink lace and ribbons, or a little boy with sparkling eyes, mischievous grin, and a cleft in his chin. You'll play catch with him and attend all his games. Of course, he'll be the star player. Incidentally, you'll have infinite patience, you'll never let yourself go no matter how little sleep you get, and you'll be a constant resource for fun, games, traditions, and educational activities. You'll be—da da da da—Supermom!

Before you know it, darling little baby samples begin to arrive in the mail, complete with coupons for a staggering array of items you simply must have with a baby on the way. A complimentary issue of some great expectations parenting/pregnancy magazine finds its way into your hands, and you're doomed. Not necessarily by the articles—although the umpteenth checklist you read for what to take to the hospital and what you *must* have before you bring baby home is certainly overwhelming—but by the advertisements. Many of them show blissful, well-rested mothers seated in polished walnut rocking chairs, cradling their sleeping infants and wearing white peignoir sets. White! Can you believe it? Where are the models who were sent home with Tucks, Preparation H, and diapers for big people? Where are the bleary-eyed mothers who stumble sleepily, if not resentfully, to the nursery and who stub their toes on the changing table and have bed head and dream of long hours of uninterrupted sleep?

People who tell moms-to-be stories are divided into two camps. The Haves and the Have Nots. The Haves advocate getting an epidural, preferably in your eighth month. No need to experience any discomfort. The Have Nots are adamantly opposed to any form of pain relief whatsoever and tell you that if you will just take natural childbirth classes (if trying to push a creature that feels like an octopus through an opening the size of an ant's footprint can be called natural!), breathe well, and focus on a small stuffed bear, you'll breeze through the experience. It becomes a sick competition.

And then there's the whole hospital stay. Whether or not you deliver, if you go to a hospital to pick up your infant, people will want to visit. And no new mom truly looks her best after this ordeal. Stress, sleeplessness, hard physical labor, the sheen of sweat, and the fluctuating hormones are all prohibitive factors. You want people to rejoice with you, but you can't reconcile the woman you see in the mirror with the one in the magazines. The one exception I have encountered is my friend Anna. She adopted her infant son, Bo, and took him to Sam's Club at two days old, wearing a very slim-fitting pair of blue jeans. She did it just to gloat. She was accosted by a woman with a similarly young infant who demanded to know Bo's age. "Two days," Anna replied sweetly. She was forced to admit that Bo was adopted when the woman tried to shove her into the deep freeze.

Once you get home and all settled in—no snickering, please—things will get better, you tell yourself. You'll establish a routine, get the baby on a feeding schedule, and life will return to normal with the addition of one angelic infant. (Does anyone else think homicidal thoughts when confronted with the phrases "Slept like a baby" or "As easy as taking candy from a baby"? They sure didn't mean a toddler on that last one, did they!)

And then all baby poop breaks loose. We find ourselves conversing with pediatricians, our parents, complete strangers, and even our husbands about the color and consistency of the baby's bowel movements. We learn the BRAT diet for plugging (bananas, rice, applesauce, toast) and all about the thermometer and Vaseline or strained plums trick for unplugging. We applaud ourselves for taking a shower before noon, and our brain cells seem to have deteriorated at an alarming rate. When did we sleep last anyway?

Some demented medical textbook writer had the bizarre idea of something called a six-week checkup, at which time you are approved to resume the activities that began this journey in the first place. I nearly passed out when I discovered my husband circled this date on his calendar with a smiley face. Even those who haven't given birth physically are still emotionally and physically exhausted. New moms, given the choice between sex and sleep, choose sleep nearly every time.

Confessions of a Supermom

Strangely, if you decide to take the plunge and become a stay-at-home, the delusions of grandeur and Supermom syndrome increase. By gosh, you once handled an outside career, your home, husband, kids, and personal life, so you ought to be a whiz at handling this at-home stuff! Or so the thought process goes.

Stephanie, formerly my baby sister's best friend and an obnoxious pest when we were kids, is now also *my* friend by virtue of that great equalizer, motherhood. When I told her about this book and the title of this chapter, she gave me permission to share her story.

When she announced, one week prior to delivering her second child, that she was retiring from teaching, her colleagues responded with shock and some derision. "You'll never make it! You're too career-oriented. Are you crazy?" Her response was one brave statement: "I'm going to be Supermom."

She writes,

> I had read plenty of books, magazines, and articles by Supermoms, about Supermoms, and for Supermoms. I was armed with an arsenal of arts and crafts activities, fingerplays, storybooks, and loving discipline. I knew how to organize a toy room, stretch the

grocery budget, and teach ABCs. I could leap potty chairs in a single bound. I just hadn't read about kryptonite.

Kryptonite entices you to serve your children Pop-Tarts and milk in front of the Disney Channel every morning while you sneak back to bed for another 30 minutes of sleep. Kryptonite plagues you with hobbies that take time away from your children. Kryptonite addicts you to soap operas so that you rush the children to nap time without reading them a book. Fortunately, even kryptonite supplies occasionally run low.

Stephanie recounts the tale of a day when she sought to spin a little magic. She hopped into a kryptonite-free shower and emerged as Supermom! She wanted to tell her three-year-old about the pirate movie she'd watched the night before but realized the word *pirate* meant nothing to her. So, being Supermom, she buried 30 pennies in the sandbox she'd built for the kids on a previous kryptonite-free day. She created a play path of swings, slides, and toy cars along the way to the sandbox.

"Sidney!" Stephanie ran down the hall with her freshly drawn treasure map complete with sample pennies. "Look what I found on the doorstep!" (Supermom is allowed to stretch the truth a bit.) She showed her the map and asked her where she thought the treasure might be buried. Sidney eagerly figured out the map and dragged her little brother out the back door, down the slide, past the car, through her swing set, and to the buckets. "How did the pirates know red is my favorite color, Mommy?" She had labeled one bucket for each child at the corner of the sandbox. Smart kid. Smart Supermom.

After five minutes of digging, Sidney began to lose interest. It is *hard* to find pennies buried in sand. Stephanie recalls,

> I dug. And I dug. No pennies. Sidney dug. JT dug. The dog dug. But no pennies. I made an excuse to run inside, grabbed more pennies, and dashed back to treasure island. Unfortunately, my Supermom powers were wearing off by this time, so as I tried to drop the new pennies on top of the sand, Sidney saw them fall from my hands. I wanted to cry.

But Sidney's superpowers are far superior to my own. She dove for the pennies and filled her bucket with them. Then she said, "Watch, Mommy! I can take them from my bucket and bury them and pretend to find them again!" She buried and reburied her pennies all morning.

Stephanie learned the lesson: "Don't bury pennies in the sand. They're impossible to find. Oh, and even Supermom has less than Marvel Hero days."

I laughed and laughed when I read her tale. If we could all have one great big mommy sleepover together we'd never run out of such stories, and amazingly enough, we're always up for another adventure as soon as the kryptonite wears off.

Don't forget to ask God to help you recognize your kryptonite tendencies. Learn to rely on Him rather than attempt so many things in your own strength.

Some things about motherhood you just have to experience for yourself. I know of no other job that is so aggravating, mind-boggling, frustrating, rewarding, and joyful at the same time. It seems impossible that a woman can feel competent and like a dismal failure at the same job, sometimes on the same day. But it's true.

That said, don't for one second underestimate the value of what you do. Nor should you trick yourself into thinking that anyone else could do what you do any better than you can do it. God placed you in this home with this family for His purpose. And He *is* a superhero!

A Mother's Influence

Moms are necessary. They glue a family together. They serve as a buffer in conflicts. As a safety during rough tackles. They create memories and organize fun. They plan vacations, experiment at dinnertime, and can belt out a mean rendition of "Where the Boys Are" with only a curling iron for a microphone. They model motherhood and marriage for their children. They encourage dreams and, at just the right moment, pray for the strength to let go long enough so their children can achieve them.

This mommy stuff isn't over after our children hit kindergarten either. "Once a mother, always a mother," says my mother. I'm beginning to agree. "We used to think that the most critical time to stop working was when our children were babies and toddlers. But new research suggests that adolescence is when our kids need us most," writes Carol Lynn Mithers in an article entitled, "The New Stay-at Home Mom."[1]

Today, many moms are mothering toddlers, even infants, at the same time they are mothering kids on the threshold of puberty. That brings about a whole new need for superpowers, or at least good detective skills. The infant cooing you once interpreted now morphs into a series of grunts that are just as essential to translate. Yet we sometimes miss this opportunity: "75 percent of parents of 9-year-olds report 'high or moderate involvement' in their child's school-related activities. [At] age 14, only 55 percent of parents are still that involved, and with each passing year, the rate continues to drop."[2]

I have witnessed this myself as a room mother in three different classrooms with one baby still at home. Whichever child is in kindergarten is flooded with room-mother volunteers. My third-grader's class has significantly fewer volunteers. At the middle-school level, room parents were virtually nonexistent. We do ourselves a disservice when we flood our children with time and attention during their baby years and then slack off as they grow.

Teens who have a good relationship with their parents are less likely than their peers to smoke and drink. Feeling connected to their families "(which not only meant feeling loved but having a parent present before or after school, at bedtime or dinner) helped protect teens against almost every health-risk behavior studied, according to the National Longitudinal Study on Adolescent Health, which studied more than 12,000 girls and boys in grades 7-12."[3]

That's especially critical to know since "once a child enters adolescence, his risk of dying soars by 300 percent."[4] An increase in risk-taking behaviors and the drive to be accepted in their peer groups fuel such statistics. Yet studies link family time and dinners together several times per week as being one of the highest related factors of success on ACT scores. And there's more good news—according to the National Center on Addiction and Substance Abuse at Columbia University, teens who ate dinner five to seven times a week with their families were 45 percent less likely to try alcohol, 24 percent less apt to smoke marijuana, and 67 percent more likely to get A's compared to kids who never or rarely dined with their families![5]

Girls who enjoy close relationships with their mothers are less likely to attempt what experts term "early sex," and a healthy father-daughter relationship can be a huge factor in the abstinence-until-marriage equation. All of which means that, quality time aside, we're going to have to do a lot of plain old hanging around and hanging out together. I get very interesting information from my oldest daughter on long walks or in the car, much better stuff than when I attempt a foolish conversation beginning with "So, tell me about your day!" Asking open-ended questions stimulates creative thinking and evokes better answers in children of all ages; they are especially great for preteens and teenagers.

All things considered, we at-home mothers have a wonderful job. A high calling indeed. Believe it or not, we're sometimes the subject of envy! "77 percent of moms who hold full-time jobs outside the home say they would stay home full time if they could."[6] Don't get into a competition or a judgment fest with moms who work outside the home. We desperately need each other; both groups long to be Supermom and both are uncannily susceptible to kryptonite. At the same time, don't let naysayers detract from your attempts at being Supermom, even during a weak moment when you're being bombarded by kryptonite.

Author and teacher Tony Campolo says his wife has an excellent comeback for people who condescendingly ask what it is moms do all day: "I am socializing two Homo sapiens into the dominant values of the Judeo-Christian tradition in order that they might be instruments for the transformation of the social order into the kind of eschatological utopia that God willed from the beginning of creation." Tony reports that often she would look at the person who had asked and inquire sweetly, "And what is it that YOU do?" Frequently the reply, "Uh, I'm a lawyer," was made in a very subdued voice.[7]

Still wondering? Dr. James Dobson summarized some recent findings from a study led by Dr. Burton White at the Harvard University's Preschool Project. The team studied children aged eight to eighteen months over a ten-year period. Guess what? "The single most important environmental factor in the life of the child is his mother....Mom carries more influence on her child's experiences than any other person or circumstance."[8] Sounds like Supermom stuff to me!

Together we can deflect crises, build block towers, leap them with a single bound, shape self-esteem, and mold dreams. While we're at it, we can teach philosophy, nurture the future, deflect far flung Lego creations from hitting the sleeping baby, and quiz children on spelling words, make dinner, talk on the phone, and kick the dryer door shut with our foot at the same time. Oh, and we could do it while nursing the baby if we had to. Supermoms of the world unite!

QUESTIONS FOR STUDY AND REFLECTION

1. Did your vision of motherhood match well with the reality? Why or why not? What have been the most difficult adjustments for you?

2. What things are kryptonite for you? List them. By doing so, you rob them of much of their power. Now pray over them.

3. There is power in simple gestures. Read 1 Samuel 2:19. Each year Samuel's mother, Hannah, made him a little robe and took it to him when she and Elkanah would travel to offer the annual sacrifice. Not only did she remember her promise to give Samuel back to God, but she let her son know that he was ever in her thoughts.

What are some small but powerful gestures you've done or are doing with or for your child? What impact do you think they could have on his future?

4. For good or for evil, mothers have great influence over their children. Read Genesis 25:28. "Isaac…loved Esau, but Rebekah loved Jacob." Such favoritism became kryptonite for Rebekah. Read the account in Genesis 27:2-13. Rebekah eavesdropped. She encouraged Jacob to participate in deceit and trickery, thus beginning a long feud between the brothers and doubtless harming her husband's trust in her. In contrast, Moses' mom, Jochebed, trusted God not only for her son's safekeeping but for his future role in saving the Israelites from the cruelty of the Egyptians. What a contrast! Have you ever, even by example, encouraged your children in a "white lie"? For example, when they pick up the phone, you've said to your child, "Tell them I'm not here." Have you ever used your children to manipulate your husband? Prayerfully consider your role as the keeper of their spiritual future. Describe a time when you have actively trusted God for something in your child's life, or perhaps for that life itself.

5. Read Psalm 113:9. What word is used to describe a mother?

    _____

    Read Isaiah 66:13. What word picture is used to describe how God comforts us? _____

    _____

    Read 1 Thessalonians 2:7. In what way does Paul describe the apostles' actions at Thessalonica?

6. Read Psalm 63:6. When you're awakened in the middle of the night to tend to a sick child or because worry has whispered in on the wings of your dreams, what is your response? How could you make it a better one if needed?

7. When kryptonite threatens you, read Psalm 94:18-19. Now read verse 17 too. Who gives us help? Fill in these blanks:

"When I said, 'My _____ is _____,' your _____ Oh LORD, _____ me. When _____ was great within me, your _____ brought _____ to my soul."

8. What would happen to our self-reliance if we truly remembered God was in control? How would that affect our mothering?

Action Plan

On the next kryptonite-free day you experience, jot down all the factors that reduced kryptonite's siren call. Learn from those factors. Now, plan a wonderful, structured kryptonite-free play day in which you are fully involved with your children. Make sure to be flexible as you hear their desires too.

Journal

Briefly write down a memory paragraph about the first moment you found out you were expecting a baby, whether it was a placement call from the adoption agency, or a positive pregnancy test. Read back over your memories and recall those feelings. Deliberately dwell on the sweetness and the overwhelming sense of blessed responsibility. Ask God to bring that to your mind each day.

Memorize

Say this about your children: "What is our hope, our joy, or the crown in which we will glory in the presence of our Lord Jesus when he comes? Is it not you?" (1 Thessalonians 2:19).

Chapter 3

Maximizing Your Day

A house is who you are,
not who you ought to be.

—*Jill Robinson*

I still have the snapshot. You can find it buried in the back of an as-yet-unscrapbooked photo album. My oldest daughter, then seven, took this picture of me in what she called my "Samantha" dress in honor of the beautifully outfitted housewife of *Bewitched* fame. It was a lime-green, linen, belted shirt-dress that fairly screamed, "I am an early 1960s housewife wannabe!"

The picture was taken at 8:01 AM on my first official day as a bona fide stay-at-home mom. By 8:07 I looked like a dryer sheet that had been used for more than ten loads. (Why did no one tell me linen wrinkled so quickly?) Still, I determined not to let that bother me, and I managed most of my goals for the day: aerobics, a quick Bible study, one-on-one time with each child, a loving call to my spouse at work, and the preparation of what I hoped would be the first of many stunning home-cooked meals. After all, I was at home now. Full time. I had just gained seven extra hours in my day! Oh, the things I could do! (Why are you laughing?)

For dinner, I made chicken-salad tomato stars by slicing tomatoes open to resemble star shapes and plopping tender scoops of chicken salad into each and placing them on crisp lettuce leaves surrounded by grapes and a side of baked chips. "That looks cute, Cinso!" my husband praised me. "Where's dinner?"

My ambitious routine lasted for two more days. I quickly learned my husband would almost always want something that at least resembled beef for dinner. The linen dress found a new home in the children's dress-up box. And the extra seven hours I thought I'd find? I have no idea where they went.

I begin every seminar I lead on the home by having this sentiment on the screen as women are filing in:

Lions or Gazelles?

Every morning in Africa, a gazelle wakes up.
It knows it must run faster than the fastest lion,
Or it will be killed.
Every morning a lion wakes up.
It knows it must outrun the slowest gazelle
Or it will starve to death.
It doesn't matter whether you are a lion or gazelle:
When the sun comes up, you'd better be running.

—Author unknown

We are instantly bonded, whether or not we work outside the home, because that's exactly how we feel. As women, wives, workers, friends, nurturers, or homemakers, we're either hunting for something or we are being hunted. In fact, the number one home-related stress according to

women I've talked to all across the country is the frustrating lack of organization in their days since they've stayed home.

"I'm so busy all day. I am just exhausted by the time my husband gets
home, but most of the time I can't point to anything specific I've truly
accomplished!" This is a statement I hear repeated in various forms at
conference after conference and among my own friends who are employed
at home. How does the professional mom maximize her day? How does
she seize the day, instead of allowing it to seize her—and then shake her
hard?

There are far too many books on my shelf about time management,
housecleaning, and organizational skills. Some of them I've yet to read.
So why did I buy them? Because I was seduced by wonderful covers,
sensational promises, and gorgeous pictures. Sigh. Most of the thicker
volumes are too specific and too involved and are therefore unrealistic for
me. I'm guessing it's the same for many of you. So, in the next couple of
chapters I'm going to attempt a *Reader's Digest* version for all of us who
are not that thrilled about cleaning or organizing and would rather do
other things. My goals are to…

1. provide a template for an enjoyable, productive day.
2. help you get organized enough to feel your day has accomplished
   much.
3. prevent you from drowning in clutter or being strangled by an overcommitted schedule.
4. assist you in carving out spaces for yourself during the day.
5. suggest some basic tools and principles you can adapt to fit your
   needs.

The Weekly Overview

Once a week my husband and I try to coordinate our schedules and
fill each other in on upcoming events. This has prevented more than a

few unpleasant surprises, and it is always easier to deal with dinners if I know he's going to be late on certain evenings.

Once a week I try to plot my week too. I have certain chores I've committed to doing on certain days; other tasks are seasonal or occasional. By formulating a plan for how to accomplish general goals I have, my days are usually more productive than they would otherwise be. The key to creating the sense of organization is to divide and conquer. Use one of the daily-planner sheets in the back of this book, design your own, or just use a beautifully decorated, lined notebook. Find one of those darling beaded ones—a fun lift in a day filled with chores.

Below is a sample of my weekly chore division and daily breakdown.

Sunday	Sunday school, church, afternoon—rest, scrapbook, read, family night
Monday	Grocery shopping AM
Tuesday	Writing day, library day, Greg does bathrooms PM
Wednesday	Errands, Bible study PM
Thursday	Dust, vacuum entire house, afternoon women's Bible-study group
Friday	Change sheets, mow lawn AM
Saturday	Free Day!

Notes: I do some laundry almost every day. With a family of six, it's just too overwhelming not to stay caught up. Also, I do daily maintenance sweeps. If you go to bed with your kitchen clean and your family room picked up, life is much easier to face the next day.

You may want to institute a shoes-off-at-the-door policy. Studies show that 80 percent of the dirt in our homes comes from the bottom of our shoes! And that's without mentioning some of the more disgusting things our shoes have stepped in.

Daily Time Schedule (Sample from a Tuesday)	
7:00 AM	Get up, dress, oversee children getting ready, breakfast
7:40 AM	Leave home, Eden to middle school, Emmy to elementary school, Ellie to preschool Notes: Eden needs lunch, Emmy—show and tell
8:00 AM	Devotions on porch, aerobics
9:00 AM	Make grocery list, plan menu, play with Elexa
10:00 AM	Errands: dry cleaner, post office, drop off book to Mom's, groceries, stop at park to swing!
11:15 AM	Pick Ellie up from preschool, sign up for party snacks
12:00 PM	Lunch and stories, rock Elexa
1:00 PM	Laundry and dishes, nap for 45 minutes
2:00 PM	Answer correspondence, girls' naps, work on presentation, read, and relax
3:00 PM	Pick up Eden and Emmy from school
4:00 PM	Eden to piano lessons, Emmy and Ellie to library
5:00 PM	Start dinner, return phone calls

Time-Savers to Help Your Day

If you have school-age children, try this wonderful weekly time-saver: Every Sunday afternoon, choose a week's worth of clothing for each child, allowing them to give input if they want to. One of the best recent investments I made was $20 for a hanging canvas organizer that attaches with Velcro loops around the center of my middle girls' closet rod. It has five cubbyholes, labeled for each day of the week. At the bottom are two spots for shoes. In an unhurried fashion we are able to select school- and weather-appropriate clothes. It saves time in the mornings. It virtually ends arguing about what to wear. By having everything laid out in advance, I'm not scrambling during a rushed school morning trying to remember whether or not it's PE day and who does and doesn't have to wear tennis shoes. Lillian Vernon catalogs, Better Living Stores, and Target all have these organizers.

If you don't plan your day, circumstances will surely plan it for you. Therefore, one of the most important factors is to begin plotting your day the night before. One of the worst enemies of organization is the feeling of being overwhelmed: *I don't know where to start!* A to-do list gives you a plan of attack.

Having a written visual also accomplishes two more things: 1) It allows you the immense emotional satisfaction of drawing a line through a finished task. 2) It provides a defined beginning and ending to each day. By reviewing and adding to your lists at night you can help eliminate the near-constant running list that scrolls down most female brains at night, preventing them from falling asleep.

Pour bowls of cereal and lay out vitamins the night before. For simplicity during school mornings, we usually alternate Pop-Tarts with Cheerios and toast with sweetened cereals. Friday is our special breakfast day. Then we'll have sausage/egg/cheese bake, waffles, and bacon or homemade muffins with fruit salad.

Post the school lunch menu where it can be easily seen. Ours is on the fridge door. The day the menu comes home, the girls choose which days they want to eat at school. Eden circles her choices, Emmy draws a square around hers, and Ellie draws a line with highlighter underneath. I can easily tell who needs a lunch and who's eating at school. Write a check that covers each child's school meals at the beginning of each month. Pack lunches at night too. While you're at it, pack a note in your child's lunch. Eden often says this is a highlight of her day; Emmy and Ellie have saved most of theirs. Hallmark makes an inexpensive line of kid cards. Hearts at Home makes lunchbox notes, and Focus on the Family Resources offer Hugs in a Lunchbox. Or make or stamp your own little messages.

Make the Most of Mornings

The last thing I want to do is burden you with yet another mandate in your already packed days. However, I want to urge you to begin your day with God. Stretch and pray as you open your eyes, thankful you are here to greet another day. Keep a flip calendar with a scripture and a devotional thought on your bedside table or bathroom counter. Meditate on each verse as you prepare for your day. Let Him in on every aspect of your life.

For all moms, but especially brand-new moms, I recommend taking your bath or shower at night. I also advise making your bed first thing when you get out of it. That way, no matter how messy or crazy your day, there is always an oasis.

If you have infants or very young children, mornings are usually the best time for running errands or doing household tasks. Take advantage of the golden hours before the cranky pre-nap phase sets in. Infants are usually very content in their carriers where they can see you working. Baby swings or a blanket on the floor are other great alternatives. Toddlers and preschoolers love to help dust or even help vacuum. But on the balky days when they aren't in the mood to be mommy's little helpers, try these quick alternatives to a videotape for distraction while you work.

+ Create a virtually indestructible picture book by cutting out magazine pictures of animals, familiar household objects, babies, food, blocks, books, snowflakes, trees, and oceans and placing them in a simple photo album. I began making our book with my first child, and we have added to it with each girl. We are now "reading" this book with our fourth! It is a sure-fire way to buy enough time to do a few quick tasks.

+ When preschool children are missing older siblings who have gone to school, give them an index card with an uppercase and lowercase letter of the alphabet and a picture of something beginning with that sound. Since even my stick figures are barely recognizable, I stuck to things like balls, apples, suckers, and rocks. I put a different card by their breakfast bowl once a week. Then all day, whether running errands or looking at picture books, you can keep an eye out for that letter.

+ Trace your child's foot for a pattern and make 26 feet, one for each letter of the alphabet. Use masking tape to fix them to the floor, following the route you'll be cleaning. Hand him a flashlight to follow each letter, and be available to help him say the letters out loud.

Make the Most of Afternoons

The average child's nap time, which I got by polling hundreds of moms, is two hours. Use nap time wisely! If you're lucky enough to make this average, allow me to share a game plan for making this a halcyon time! If you need a nap, then by all means take one—guilt free! But take it *first*. If you wait to lie down until your myriad of little chores are done, you'll never get any rest. The only exception to this might be to start a load of laundry and run the dishwasher, so some of your work is being done for you while you rest.

Go ahead. Grab a new magazine or the book you've been dying to read and crawl up on your freshly made bed. Pull a cozy quilt over you, set your alarm for 45 minutes. Read just enough to feel relaxed and drowsy. Now—sleep, glorious sleep! When your alarm goes off, you'll still have an hour and 15 minutes. Use 30 minutes to straighten the house, unload the dishwasher, fold the clothes—any chores that you can accomplish so much more rapidly without sweet little hands following you around undoing it. If you're caught up on chores, you might want to use this for your devotional or exercise time. Use your remaining 30 to 45 minutes to do something that relaxes you, inspires you, or motivates you.

If you've been up all night with a sick baby or a toddler who wet the bed—or a preschooler with bad dreams—sleep until those sweet voices on the baby monitor demand your presence. If it's a cloudy, rainy day, or a snowy, drizzling day, sleep the whole time too. For a precious treat, bring your little one to bed with you, curl around them, and sleep. There's nothing like waking up to a rosy-cheeked toothless baby grin or a toddler's warm, sleepy smile! My children are often amazed that when they wake up, the cranky mommy has been replaced by a refreshed, smiling mommy.

If you have school-age children, make homecomings an event. Sit down with them around the table and look at all of their worksheets and art projects. Choose some for refrigerator display and some to send to grandparents or share with nursing-home residents or soldiers overseas. Serve a light snack and visit with them. This 15 or so minutes of uninterrupted attention can go a long way toward making your afternoon go more smoothly.

Ask open-ended questions that can't be answered yes or no, such as "What was the best part of your day?" "If today had a color, what would it be? Why?" "What's the favorite thing you learned today?" I'll never forget what Jackina Stark says of this ritual in her book *Framing a Rainbow*. Her daily habit was to invite her girls, "Come share your lives with me." Wow.

Immediately sign all permission slips, book order forms, notes from the teacher, and so on, and return them to the backpacks so everything is in order for the next day.

If you home school, it is equally important that the stopping place for your day be a point of minor celebration. Stop for snacks, bake something together, or prepare dinner together. Or have one of the children read aloud to you while you cook.

When you get the hang of it, maximizing your day will be second nature to you, much as other good, productive habits are. It takes approximately 21 days for any lifestyle change to become permanent. Look at Mom Aid #1 for some tools and tricks to help you make and keep those habits.

The Family Manager's Creed

I oversee a small organization—
Where hundreds of decisions are made daily,
Where property and resources are managed,
Where health and nutritional needs are determined,
Where finances and futures are discussed and debated,
Where projects are planned and events are arranged,
Where transportation and scheduling are critical,
Where team-building is a priority,
Where careers begin and end.
...I am a Family Manager.

Kathy Peel, *The Family Manager*

This year I decided I would be committed to doing my devotions and also my aerobics before the busy day gets underway. I've learned a valuable lesson, perhaps just for the purpose of writing these chapters. The times when I have stuck to those goals, I have accomplished just as much, if not more, than when I allow other things to fill my day. My energy and inner peace are available in much greater quantities. I am more patient and more upbeat. Hmmm...perhaps God is trying to tell me something.

Keeping the Right Perspective

Realize that the suggestions and offerings in these chapters are just principles. They represent what an *ideal* day might look like. I want to offer two disclaimers. First, this is how my days and weeks go when everything falls into place. I don't want to open hate mail from women who read my books and then erroneously believe that this is what the Dagnan household looks like and sounds like every single day. No. My

house is just like yours. Some days I've been up all night with the baby
and I don't have the energy to do anything. Some days I'm cranky and do
everything, but without much tenderness and with a lot of noise! Some
days my perfect plans collapse because all of the children are home and
wired to the max, thrilled by an unexpected snow day. Some days interruptions, spills, lost things, and broken appliances intrude.

Second, don't ever allow any schedule, no matter how carefully
planned, to derail you from the real reason you stay home—to be there for
your children. Be flexible and build extra time into your plans. Children
don't like to always be hurried. (Come to think of it, we don't either.)

Make sure your errands include some dawdle time to allow for
the unexpected and for little drops of joy. This morning I had to run
some clothes to my mom's house so they could dry in her dryer. Our
dryer is broken and it's 30 degrees outside with a winter storm warning, so I wasn't really up for the clothesline thing. On the way back, I
stopped at the store to pick up a roll of developed film and grab a few
bags of candy for the children's Valentine parties. I wanted to get in and
out quickly. Two-year-old Elexa Rose had other ideas. She patted every
stuffed animal in the place. She oohed and aahed over the shiny hearts
hanging from the ceiling. She handed me her coat with an impish grin.
"Too hot, Mama!" she said, and took off running. I chased. She giggled.
I stood at the end of the aisle and announced firmly it was time to check
out. Right now. "Looking at cards, Mama," she replied in that tiny voice
with the cheerful lilt.

I took a moment to look at that aisle from her perspective. It looked
fun. Rows and rows of colorful, shiny, glittering, perfectly folded greeting
cards. Matching envelopes to boot. Ribboned gift sacks, rolls of pink, red,
and white wrapping paper, perfect for wielding like swords. A stuffed bear
or three-dimensional heart thrown in here and there for good measure.
So I waited for her to finish. Then we held hands and paid for our things,
and I let her hold the sack like a "big girl." Her tiny fingers were warm and
wiggling in mine. Her face looked up at me with that pure delight only

a child has, and everything on my schedule faded into its proper place—into the background.

QUESTIONS FOR STUDY AND REFLECTION

1. Using the T chart below, compare and contrast benefits and features of your day as a working mom and as a stay-at-home mom.

Working	Staying at Home

2. The author feels that time with God and time for yourself are both keys to maximizing your day. Do you agree? Discuss how both things might "lengthen" the hours of your day. If possible, share about a time when being obedient to what God wanted from you actually seemed to increase your productivity.

3. Read John 6:1-15, Mark 8:1-13, and Luke 5:15-16. What did Jesus do when pressure got to Him? Fill in the blanks from Luke 5:16: "Jesus often _____ to _____ places and _____."

4. Read through the gospel of Luke during the next few weeks. Make note of Jesus' interaction with people. Write down what you think His top three priorities were.

5. Read Psalm 84:5,7. What pilgrimage is being spoken of? How does the idea of going from "strength to strength" renew your heart for the tasks at hand?

6. Do you see yourself as a lion or a gazelle? Why?

7. Which is harder for you to include on a typical day—time for prayer and devotions, or time for yourself? List your top priorities. Now chart your days and check your calendar. Does the way you're spending your time match up with your priorities? If not, actively work to create a better balance.

Action Plan

Have you ever noticed how what you don't plan for tends to happen anyway? This week try the weekly overview plan. Spend some time thinking through your list of chores, errands, church activities, social plans, and children's extracurricular activities. How could you best divide and conquer this list? Is there anything you could pare down or eliminate?

After the birth of my fourth child, something had to give. I eliminated singing in the church choir, got a little more organized, and decided that my standards of cleanliness at home could be much lower. I can live with a little dirt as long as everything is picked up!

Choose one of the six "tools and tricks" in Mom Aid #1 to implement this coming week. (No, type A's, you may not try all six this week, or even this month. Pace yourself.)

Journal

Plot your ideal day. What kinds of things do you see yourself accomplishing? Enjoying? Of course *all* days can't be ideal, but what typically holds you back from at least being close to that goal?

Memorize

"Choose for yourselves this day whom you will serve, whether the gods your forefathers served...But as for me and my household, we will serve the LORD" (Joshua 24:15).

Chapter 4

Taking Back
Your Time

*Lost, yesterday somewhere between
sunrise and sunset, two golden hours,
each set with sixty diamond minutes.
No reward is offered,
for they are gone forever.*

—Horace Mann

Although she is speaking of writing and writer's block, I adore Anne Lamott's formula for days when she can't seem to get any work done. "To live as if I am dying...time is so full for people who are dying in a conscious way, full in the way that life is for children. They spend big round hours. So...I say to myself, 'Okay, hmmm, let's see. Dying tomorrow. What should I do today?'"

Your time with your children is exactly that important. You get only one shot at creating the atmosphere in which they will grow, the values they will adopt, the example they will emulate, and the memories they will forever carry with them. For that reason, you need to be in charge of your time.

Would an outsider watching you be able to figure out your priorities by observing how you spend your time? If asked about our priorities, most of us could verbalize the correct answer: God, spouse, family, church, work—but most of our schedules don't reflect this.

Scripture has set forth principles about stewardship, and I think they apply to our resources, talents, and times (see Matthew 25:14-29). And a comforting thought about our days too: "My times are in your hands" (Psalm 31:15).

Jesus Himself set an excellent example. He was all about prioritizing His time. In His short 33 years on this earth, He recognized and accomplished His goals.

+ *Ministry*. He preached, healed, raised the dead, and comforted the hurting. He gave hope to the hopeless, rewarded the faithful, and gave second chances at life to the spiritually dead.

+ *Relationships*. He spent time with His friends, introducing them to His Father. He went with them to weddings, parties, and impromptu picnics. He fished with them and shared meals with them. He reached out to friends and enemies alike. His love for people was evident in everything He did.

+ *Doing the will of His Father*. He spent time in prayer and time alone, renewing His strength for the rigors of life and the trials and temptations He encountered. He fulfilled His Father's will ultimately by giving His life on the cross.

+ *He recognized His physical body had limits*. He was God, but in human form. He escaped out on the boat, to the garden, and up on the mountain for prayer, alone time, and time with friends. If Jesus needed those things, then what in the world makes us believe we are any different?

Consider with me for a moment if you might need some assistance in taking back your time.

Symptoms of a Disorganized Life

1. Desk takes on cluttered appearance

2. Car is dirty, cluttered, and poorly maintained

3. Lowered self-esteem

4. Forgotten appointments and messages

5. Energy invested in unproductive tasks

6. Feel poorly about quality of work

7. Procrastination

8. Quality of personal relationships suffers

9. Feelings of general dissatisfaction

—Adapted from *Ordering Your Private World*,
Gordon MacDonald

Do you have any of those symptoms? Ever have days when you feel like you've been run over by a Mack truck? Or worse, wish you could've been? Claim two or three of these wonderful promises on a Mack-truck day—and then, armed with the truth of His strength, tackle your day with gusto!

- "Come to me all you who are weary and burdened, and I will give you rest"(Matthew 11:28).

- "My power is made perfect in weakness"(2 Corinthians 12:9).

- "You will keep in perfect peace him whose mind is steadfast, because he trusts in you" (Isaiah 26:3).

- "He himself is our peace" (Ephesians 2:14).

Secrets to Squelching Stress

Multitask. Not so much that you can't live in the moment, though. Relax and enjoy a movie, but if it helps you, by all means use the commercial breaks for whipping up a snack, folding a load of laundry, or answering a letter. Cross-stitch or knit or whatever else thrills your soul as you watch. Write a quick note of encouragement or browse recipe books for this week's menu while you're on hold. Tape your prayer list to the steering wheel or dash of your car so you can pray at stoplights or as you're driving along.

Cordless phones are wonderful inventions. They enable us to roam around watching our children as we talk. We can also fold clothes, file our nails, sort paper stacks, straighten a junk drawer, and start dinner while we talk. Most now come equipped with a speakerphone feature or an earpiece.

Busy basket. This is my number-one sanity-saver with all the time I spend in the car, waiting in the car, waiting at doctor's appointments, waiting for someone to finish ballet, gymnastics, or piano. Waiting for the train to cross. Waiting for the children to actually come *out* of the school building. In my busy basket I keep a supply of little notecards for answering correspondence and dashing off notes of encouragement, a Bible, a small notebook, a supply of Post-It notes for jotting down thoughts or reminders, a magazine, and a book to read. I leave this basket in the car, so I'm never without it when I'm unexpectedly stuck. But it's easily portable for taking into meetings and waiting rooms.

Up your energy with exercise. I know, I know—and I can hear the groans. However, if you can aim for walking two miles a day or do 30 minutes of aerobics four to five days a week, and lift weights twice a week, the energy benefits will be so worth it. And as a side benefit, here's great news: If you're overweight, sleeping habits improve and energy levels increase with a loss of just five to ten pounds. Drink that water too. If you drink one or more regular Cokes per day, eliminating regular sugared soda from your diet can result in a loss of ten pounds in a year. We'll look more closely at exercise later on.

Do grocery-shopping and other errands at odd hours. Grocery-shop first thing in the mornings after dropping older children at school. Better yet, if you can, hit an all-night center after the children are in bed. I often do that in the summer, and my cell phone always rings at least once. It's my bewildered husband, worried about me. Nothing's wrong—I'm just having an absolute ball, shopping and browsing without anyone wailing, begging, or whacking another sibling on the head with a box of cereal!

Double up errands. For example, you can buy stamps from the ATM machine when you have to make a deposit. Others like both online banking and purchasing stamps online.

Plan appointments wisely. Schedule doctor appointments and dental visits during vacation weeks or early-out school days. If you have more than one child, schedule as many of them as possible for the same slot at the pediatrician's office. Be forewarned, though, many offices have a limit of two children per visit. Also try to schedule your appointment as the first one in the morning or the first opening after lunch. You generally don't have to wait. Schedule your own annual physical for the week of your birthday every year. If you need follow-up visits at either a doctor's office or the beauty shop, make the next appointment before you leave.

Plan ahead. Refine your to-do list by prioritizing tasks in order of importance. Also, group errands in a logical progression according to their geographical location. For example, my errands might be...

+ drop off clothes at dry cleaners
+ return movie to rental store
+ pick up more milk, bread, and bananas
+ drop off library books
+ deposit check at bank
+ pick up special order at the bookstore

This route takes me in a rectangular loop heading back to my house—saving time and gasoline.

Utilize the word no. Remember, saying yes to something almost always involves saying no to something else. It is not necessary to explain why you cannot do something. Simply say, "I'm sorry. This is not something I can do my best with right now. Check back with me next month." Or, "I'd love to help out with that. May I bring/do/call _____ instead?" Fill in the blank with whatever works better for you. Be careful not to be insulting by saying you're too busy. So is everybody.

Consider making a list of measurable goals. In your notebook, jot down a chart with the headings: financial, spiritual, emotional, family, marriage, and personal growth. Under each heading write down your dreams for next week, next month, next year, and then five years from now. Then break down that goal into achievable baby steps. For example, one of your financial goals might be to save more. This week, you might give up having coffee at a coffee shop. Add to that and strive for saving $25 this month and so on, until you've reached your goal. Knowing where you want to be in any goal area will help you stay on track. Then when someone makes a request of you, try these tactics:

+ Don't say yes to things that don't further your goal list.
+ Recognize that *your* time is valuable too.
+ Try saying, "Let me get back to you," so you'll have time to really think it over.
+ Consider shedding one obligation before you take on another.
+ Don't accept a major new responsibility without considering how it will affect your spouse and children; discuss it with your family first.

I want to say a special word here to stay-at-home moms. It's okay for you to say no too. When I began staying home, many people thought I could run their errands, watch their children on short notice, and volunteer for everything at church and school on a grand scale. I am happy to help out on occasion, but if I said yes to every worthwhile activity, there would be no point to staying at home. Keep the reason you decided to stay at home in mind when others want to fill your time.

I know that sometimes I'm not the most popular mom at the PTA because I won't volunteer for everything. I am the room mother for each of the girls' kindergarten year. I am classroom representative another year. I attend and help bring things for each of their school parties. I usually bring things for the school carnival and work a booth at the end-of-school picnic. However, I can't handle being on a committee or chairing the fund-raising drive right now. And since the school doesn't want younger siblings along when you volunteer to help teachers in the classroom, I don't do that either. When all of my children are in school, there will be time for that.

Right now, my job is to run my home efficiently and smoothly and to be physically accessible and emotionally available to my children. No one else knows your limits or your schedule as intimately as you do. It's up to you to safeguard your time, your marriage, and your sanity.

Delegate and divide. Many women, especially we notorious perfectionist types, are terrible at delegating because we don't think anyone else can do the task like we would. And maybe we're right. So what? Wives whose husbands pitch in are generally more satisfied with their lives than those who insist on strictly segregated chores. So what if he forgets to put lotion on the baby or doesn't tape the diaper as well as you? Who cares if your ten-year-old doesn't dust items on the top shelf? Children need to learn the value of helping out. In fact, we give our children an allowance simply to teach them good budgeting skills: 10 percent goes to church, 10 percent goes in their savings account, and the rest can be spent on whatever they'd like. However, we tell them that chores are something we do just because we're part of a family, and it takes all of us to make this household work. Besides, new studies are showing that a little bit of dirt is actually healthier. When we "anti-bacterial" everything, our kids aren't being exposed to enough to boost their immune systems. (How about that for a guilt-buster? We can clean less and improve the quality of life for our precious families.)

Let every family member contribute something to dinner preparation and housecleaning. Preschool and early elementary children truly love to help. That early foundation of usefulness promotes self-esteem, as they learn that they are vital contributors to your family. You're also teaching them valuable information that prepares them for someday having homes of their own. At least that's what my mother told me when she explained why I needed to learn how to scrub toilets.

Sample of Eden's Chore Chart when we were first teaching her responsibility	
Monday	dust room
Tuesday	fold washcloths
Wednesday	set table
Thursday	help load dishwasher
Friday	set table
Daily	feed Molly, the dog bring in mail make bed straighten room

Sleep deprivation is downright dangerous, slowing reaction times, encouraging forgetfulness, increasing irritability, and lowering our immune systems. We can't be good stewards of our time when we are worn down and wrung out. Try to get as close to eight hours of sleep as possible.

Develop an attitude of gratitude. Junior and his mom, of *Veggie Tales* fame, enter our home and hearts via a CD we often play in the car. They sing a thankfulness song that is not only catchy, but *catching*, thanking the Lord for the day, for the sun, for a hug from Mom, for a lullaby....Imagine how our days might look if they were colored with genuine thankfulness for everything from buttery toast to buttery sunshine. Try creating a thankfulness journal. At the close of every day, write down a list of at least five things for which you are thankful. Sometimes your list will make you laugh. Other days, you might struggle with your list:

- I breathe well.
- The grass needs to be mowed, so it must be growing.
- My husband is snoring, so he must be here next to me, and I'm glad.
- The appliances are currently all working.
- I had plenty to eat today.

But on some days, a genuine spirit of gratitude breaks forth. *Thank You, Lord, for the mess to clean up after the party; it's wonderful to have friends over. Thank You, Lord, for the chance to rock this precious life and breathe in that wonderful baby scent, even if it is 3 AM. Thank You, Lord, that although I don't like paying bills, there is enough money to cover our expenses and needs this month. Lord, today was absolutely gorgeous! I am so glad I have health and strength to enjoy it and be productive.*

Crazy-Week Cure

We all have them. No matter how organized we become or how good our intentions, illness or a temporarily crazy season besets us. The best way I've found to combat this is to ride out the storm and tackle it during the calm. If you're overwhelmed by the mountains of laundry, piles of mail, and stacks of schoolwork that have accumulated, begin in one room and sort, toss, and put things back in their homes until that room is finished. Then move on to the next room.

If the job seems truly beyond you, set a timer for 15 minutes. That way you'll accomplish at least something, and you have a time for the task to end. Or enlist the children, set the timer, and give a coupon good for staying up 15 minutes later or choosing a movie to the one who picks up and puts away the most things before the timer dings. Finally, time yourself just once, and make note of how long it takes you to vacuum and dust the entire house. I did this once and found it takes me (when I get to do it uninterrupted) just 35 minutes to vacuum and 30 minutes to dust. In the big scheme of things, the task was not really as daunting or time consuming as I had thought.

Get in the habit of doing your chores to fun music. It energizes and lifts your spirit. Then, when you've completed your work, reward yourself with a walk outdoors, a spell on the porch with a good book, or a family trip to a drive-through for ice cream.

This is the best way to approach an overwhelming number of tasks:

"Thirty years ago my older brother, who was ten years old at the time, was trying to get a report on birds written that he'd had three months to write. [It] was due the next day. We were out at our family cabin…and he was at the kitchen table close to tears, surrounded by binder paper and pencils and unopened books on birds, immobilized by the hugeness of the task ahead. Then my father sat down beside him, put his arm around my brother's shoulder, and said, 'Bird by bird, buddy. Just take it bird by bird.' "

Anne Lamott, *Bird by Bird: Some Instructions on Writing and Life*

Getting-a-Grip Principles

There are some truths, bits of advice, and reality checks that will help you face limited time with a healthier perspective. The sooner you incorporate the following principles, the sooner you'll make peace with your schedule and bring peace into your life.

1. **Nothing will ever be completely done.** The law of motherhood adds something like these points to Murphy's Law:

- *Corollary 1:* You will never have absolutely nothing to do…
- *Corollary 2:* …because there is always something you could be doing…
- *Corollary 3:* …and because work always expands to fill the available time.

I say this not to cause you more stress, but to free you. Since it is just not possible to finish everything and then relax, just let some things go. The danger of not heeding this truth is to always live your life on hold. You know what I'm talking about: *As soon as we move into our new house, things will settle down. Life will be so much easier after the kids are potty-trained. I can get a life when the children are all in school. If my husband gets that raise, then I can stop worrying. As soon as I finish this project, I'll be able to play more.* But there will always be something, so stop just existing and start living!

2. **Remember that clutter is the sign of a life being lived.** Some of us will notice we are like cats—we have all nine lives being lived at once! By all means, use some of the tools in this book to reduce clutter, but remember that a small amount is normal. How cold would a room look without a well-loved book on the table and a cozy quilt thrown over the arm of a chair? Memories are even more important to your children than a spotless house.

3. **Forget balance.** It's no fun whirling your arms on a balance beam while juggling four grocery sacks, one toddler, and a purse the size of a Samsonite! Just live your priorities, and the rest will fall into place. There

are no perfect lives, no perfect children, no perfect marriages. Relax in the rhythm that causes you to dance, not trudge, through life.

4. **Take miniature attitude vacations.** When I was teaching high school, I hung a huge banner at the back of my classroom that read, *Attitude is the mind's paintbrush; it colors every situation.* What are your colors today? Grab five minutes and look through a photo album full of treasured memories. Bake some chocolate-chip cookies and lick the beaters. Leaf through a travel magazine and feel the sunshine on your face, the sand between your toes, and the warmth of an ocean breeze.

5. **Be flexible.** If you have children—if you have a life!—the unplanned, unexpected, and yup, even the unwanted are going to happen. If you're flexible, you'll bend; if you're rigid, you'll break.

6. **Remember that *people* are more important than things, schedules, or deadlines.** This is my heart. I live this way most of the time, but may I confess something to you? While I'm getting much better about following this than I used to be, I was a big-time backslider this morning. Twice a month, my mother graciously watches the baby so I can have two full days of uninterrupted writing time. Today was my last such day before a big deadline.

You guessed it. An unforecasted snow covered the roads. The hot-water heater quit working. My oldest daughter tripped on the stairs. My third daughter couldn't find her coat. We were late; I was frustrated. My second daughter decided she had a stomachache that was incurable. I was dubious. My husband told her that she could stay home with Mommy. I was incredulous. *On my writing day? With a deadline looming?* My first response was a selfish one. God pricked my heart. *How can you write the things you're working on this morning with that attitude?* In repentance, I gathered Emmy on my lap and told her that if she needed her mommy today, that would be just fine. If I have to write until midnight, she is still more important.

7. "Are you tired? Worn out? Come to me. Get away with me and you'll recover your life...learn the unforced rhythms of grace" (Jesus, from Matthew 11, The Message). Precious wives, mothers, and girlfriends, who among us hasn't been sand-behind-the-eyes weary? Bone-achingly weary? That unique brand of tired known as mommy-tired? Thought-about-running-away weary? Physically and emotionally exhausted? The God of All Comfort is offering no small thing: a life recovered that is brushed with the sweet oil of His gentle mercy and grace.

"Hmm, dying tomorrow. What should we do today?" We have no guarantee of anything but that our days are numbered, our breath fleeting. We have only this day. This moment. Scripture backs this up. "Show me, O LORD, my life's end and the number of my days; let me know how fleeting is my life. You have made my days a mere handbreadth; the span of my years is as nothing before you. Each man's life is but a breath" (Psalm 39:4-5).

"We're all terminal," my daddy joked when he was diagnosed with cancer just before he turned 40. "Some of us are just going sooner than others!" I'm not intending to be morbid, but rather to force us into a right perspective. *People are more important than things.* I think that concept has been somewhere in every book I have ever written, because I so want to live that way. In fact, spending our time with and for people is the best way to spend it. The reason my daddy so impacted my life and the lives of all who knew him was because he lived that way. Jesus lived that better than anyone I know. He died because of it. Aren't you so grateful?

QUESTIONS FOR STUDY AND REFLECTION

1. Read Psalm 77:11-12. How can reflecting on what we know of God and how He has helped us in the past aid us in getting through our

days? A great two-part formula for overcoming our circumstances is to 1) recall our past experiences with God and 2) concentrate on our future hope. Fill in the blank from Psalm 71:14. "As for me, I will always have _____."

2. I love the story of Esther! Read Mordecai's words to her in Esther 4:14 as she contemplates how she might use her position to help her people. What might God be able to do through you during this season of your life? Pray that He will give you unique opportunities to bless your family and others He might put in your path.

3. Read 2 Peter 3:8. When we adopt God's perspective on time, how will that change our attitudes about how we spend our time?

4. Do you have a problem with watching too much TV? Playing on the Internet? Shopping excessively? Neglecting everything while you read? Be candid with God about problem areas. Know too that it's nearly impossible to eliminate something from our "diet" of activities without filling that void with a different, more wholesome activity.

5. Waiting seems incompatible with spending time wisely. But consider Psalm 27:14. What benefits come from waiting on the Lord? From waiting in general? What is your usual response when you are forced to wait for something?

Action Plan

Actively search out ways to be still and know that He is God this week (see Psalm 46:10). Get up with the sun; lie on a blanket and stargaze. Whenever you drive somewhere, look—*really* look—around you and take in the beauty of nature, the charm of the homes you pass, and the awe of inspiring architecture. Ponder the various talents God has given people.

Journal

Write about a situation in which your hands were tied and you simply had to wait. In retrospect, list some benefits that came from that waiting period.

Memorize

"It is God who arms me with strength and makes my way perfect. He makes my feet like the feet of a deer; he enables me to stand on the heights" (Psalm 18:32-33).

Chapter 5

Making Space for Sanity

I always wanted to be someone.
I should have been more specific.

—Lily Tomlin

Twenty-one days. Once a day. Experts say that's all it takes to instill a habit. Working out. Bible reading. Relaxing. Organizing.

On the other hand, T-shirts trumpet, "A clean desk is the sign of a sick mind"; "Mess equals genius. I must be brilliant!" And depending on the day, we either want to become a "habit expert" or the poster child for sloth. We begin with gusto, tackling five new habits at once: exercising, working crosswords, taking up knitting, alphabetizing the spice rack, and conquering clutter once and for all. A few weeks later, we crash and burn. And we buy one of those tacky anti-organization tees and convince ourselves it's better. Less stressful. And let's face it—during a hectic period, it can be downright restful to enjoy a patch of "slovenliness"!

But it really isn't restful for long. And, we all have those slovenly patches that can extend their stay or even take over our homes. Together we will look at ways to keep the clutter in check so we don't obsess about it...and don't trip over it either.

"A bad habit never disappears miraculously.
It's an undo-it-yourself project."

Abigail Van Buren

Clutter Clearance

Inside and out. Mental clutter can be as big an enemy as the physical piles that so quickly accumulate. Remember the sign in my classroom? *Attitude is the mind's paintbrush; it colors every situation.* It hung there to remind me and my students that we have a choice about how we respond to our circumstances.

Simplify. A home with less physical clutter has been shown to improve relaxation, boost our moods, and derail stress. Any chance you could make do with less? Last year, on New Year's Day, I went through the house and got rid of five things from every room. That May when we lost our house in a tornado, I was very careful about what I replaced. A home that is simple can be simply beautiful and easier to maintain.

Practice two rules and one principle:

+ *The 10-second rule.* When you're getting ready to put something down, ask yourself, "Do I have ten seconds to put this where it belongs?" The answer is usually yes. So go ahead and file the bill, put up the umbrella, hang up your coat, and put the book back on the shelf. Train your family members to adopt this time-saving habit too.

+ *The 1-year rule.* If you have not worn, used, or enjoyed something in a year, get rid of it. Make a garage-sale pile, a trash pile, and a giveaway pile. When you begin storing your garage-sale items, tag and price them as you go. Keep a bag in the trunk of your car specifically for items that you will donate to Goodwill or another charity. When you decide on any item, place it immediately in the bag. That way, the next time you're near a drop-off site, everything will be ready to go. Periodically go through your book collection and take unwanted books to a secondhand bookstore. Many of them will give you cash or trade you books. I know of many who are passing their books along to friends, charities, or reselling them on eBay to earn extra income.

If you're a pack rat, a procrastinator, or just a "slow starter," it's fun to have a friend help you with this endeavor and then return the favor. An objective eye can often help you loosen your clutches on something that is worn out or outdated. Who knows? You might even have something that the other one can use.

At Christmastime, we remind our children, "You'll be getting six things for Christmas from Mommy and Daddy, grandparents, and sisters. You need to choose six things you don't play with anymore and share those with children who don't have any toys." It keeps the kids' clutter under control and serves as a reminder to them that they are indeed blessed.

♦ *The oasis principle.* Make your bed as soon as you wake up every morning. Teach your children to do the same. No matter how crazy or cluttered your day is, there will always be a spot of calm. Try to make one oasis spot in every room: the kitchen table, the coffee table, the bathroom counter, the top of the filing cabinet. Make it a habit to live by the motto "Everything has a home"— and then make sure you escort it there!

Reduce paper clutter. Only touch a piece of paper once. If it's a bill, file it or pay it. If it's a letter, go get stationery and answer it. If that's not possible, at least select a note card and address the envelope as a reminder. If it's a catalog, look through it, mark anything you want to order, place the order as soon as possible, then put it in a recycling bin or pass it on to a friend. If it's your church bulletin, write important dates on your calendar, copy down addresses of those who've recently moved or joined the church into your church directory, and clip the prayer list for the front of your Bible.

When you receive announcements, send wedding cards, baby congratulations, and sympathy cards immediately. As you finish magazines, pass them on to friends or a charity that needs current magazines. Consider saving a few in a basket just for little ones to use for crafts or school projects. Save any stickers, labels, magazine postcards (the zillions of subscription invitations that fall out of all magazines), and a few envelopes for your children to play "office" with. My kids each have a large manila envelope full of this kind of stuff and they love it. It occupies them while I'm at my desk.

Keep separate envelopes in your yearly tax file for utilities, home improvements, charitable giving, professional expenses, medical expenses, and so on. Put cancelled checks and receipts in each envelope as soon as you get them. Preparing itemized deductions at tax time will be a comparative breeze.

When kids enter school, the papers and projects pile up. I carefully choose one or two special things a week to showcase on the refrigerator. When one is replaced, it goes in a folder, by grade, in a large cardboard box for safekeeping. In general I save anything with their handprints on it, samples of the way they wrote at that age, and a few precious journal entries. At some point, choose one precious drawing from each of your children, have them sign their name to it, then add the date and frame it. I also have several of their handcrafted clay items from art class. I have a precious figurine—a self-portrait of Emmy, and a priceless lopsided bowl that was made by Eden in the second grade in which I keep my gold paperclips. They love seeing things they've made for me sitting on my desk and actually being used. Consider recycling some art projects as wrapping paper or as greeting cards or mail for nursing home residents, church shut-ins, or soldiers overseas. The girls often write personal encouraging messages on some of their artwork and send them in our care packages. Recognize that you can't save everything, though. One mother offered this tip: "Don't let young children see you throw anything they've made in the trash. Do it when they're not around and put other trash on top of it."

Storage Solutions

Establishing a proper place for your belongings is a great way to create clean spaces. Just don't use storage as an excuse to keep too much stuff. Here are ten helpful storage ideas to ease your clutter.

1. Organize a junk drawer or home-office drawer by adhering small plastic containers, stationery boxes, or vintage metal boxes of varying sizes to the bottom of the drawer with sticky-backed Velcro circles or cut-to-fit Velcro strips. (Be sure to arrange them the way you want them to be first.) Fill containers with rubber bands, buttons, paper clips, postage stamps, erasers. If you have girls, this is a great way to organize a bathroom hairbow drawer! Or thread a wide ribbon through a metal ring, attach it to a nail, and clip all the hairbows to the ribbon.

2. I love baskets, buckets, and pails! Use baskets to neatly organize diapers, wipes, extra blankets, baby paraphernalia, and small stuffed animals on changing-table shelves. In the bathroom, personalize a galvanized tin or painted metal pail with stickers that spell out each child's name. Use them for storing their hairbrush, toothpaste, lotion, bubble bath. Small buckets look neat lined up on the bathroom counter. Taller, narrower buckets painted to match a kitchen or mudroom can store each child's school papers, permission slips, and book orders.

3. Consider using baskets on or under your nightstands for holding

magazines, journals, books, lotions, and stationery. Both pretty and functional, they hold a lot without appearing cluttered.

4. If you have stairs, a stair basket is another handy investment. When you find items that need to go upstairs, place them in the stair basket and then carry the basket upstairs with you whenever you make a trip. This makes a great chore for preschool and early elementary-age children.

5. Plastic ice-cube trays are great ways to organize earrings, cuff links, and so on. They even come in fun colors now.

6. Make sure both front- and back-door entryways have pleasing, functional storage pieces. At the back door, consider hanging a peg rack for jackets, lunch boxes, and backpacks. Alternately, a coat rack with an umbrella stand at the bottom can provide the same solution for an area, using less wall space.

7. Whenever possible, purchase furniture that does double duty. For example, a storage ottoman in front of a cozy chair can hold quilts and games. We have a long storage bench in our front hallway. The inside holds umbrellas, outdoor decorative flags, jump ropes, and ball gloves. During the week, the children line up their book bags there for convenient grabbing on their way out the door.

8. Under our entryway table is a silk ivy plant (so far, I haven't killed this one) tilted on its side; next to it is a huge sturdy basket we have designated as the library basket. Everyone knows where to return their books, and the basket can be easily toted back and forth if need be.

9. A window box, painted to match your décor, makes a charming place to hold bathroom toiletries.

10. Handy and helpful car storage: I have a plastic trash container for paper trash that hooks onto a headrest. It helps keep clutter to a minimum. Another headrest is devoted to a hanging toy organizer.

Small plastic toys, crayons, and books are stored there to relieve car boredom during unexpected delays. In the trunk area of our minivan, I keep a basket containing jumper cables, a compact air compressor for flat tires, a package of wipes for the car's interior, glass-cleaning wipes to eliminate those fun fingerprints, and a can of orange-scented car freshener to use after washing and cleaning out the car. I always leave our stroller in the trunk too, so I can make an unexpected stop at the mall without having to carry my little one. Other things that come in handy are baby wipes, Kleenex, Band-Aids, Tylenol and a children's pain reliever, a flashlight, and a spare umbrella.

If you have an infant, restock the diaper bag every time you return from a trip out. Then return it to the car so you'll always have it. Always carry a bottle of infant nonaspirin pain reliever/fever reducer and a bottle of antigas drops in your diaper bag.

Quick Tips for Cleaning and Organizing

Some of these will be ideas you already use—or intend to use—while others will be just what you need to spark your imagination and organization!

+ Buy items like toothpaste, toothbrushes, toilet paper, paper towels, and deodorant either in bulk at a discount warehouse or, for small households, buy singles approximately every third trip to the store. These items don't expire and are things you always need to have on hand.

+ To save money, recycle plastic grocery bags by using them as small bathroom, bedroom, and office trashcan liners.

+ Use the phone book to make sure a store has what you need in stock before you make a trip.

+ Consider making an extra set of car keys and house keys to leave with a trusted neighbor so lockouts won't ever be a problem.

+ Worn-out flannel pajamas make great dust rags! Use a feather duster to do the job when you're running short on time. I also love the orange-scented, presoaked disposable dustcloths. They almost make dusting fun.

+ If you have two bathrooms or a two-story home, keep two separate sets of cleaning supplies.

+ A handheld vacuum is great for getting crumbs without having to lug out the big version.

+ Keep your calendar with you. Don't say yes to any commitments without consulting both it and your spouse. Rare is the commitment that doesn't affect your family too.

+ Jot down a list of things you want to talk about with people that you have to call long-distance. Keep it by the phone; it will make your calls more streamlined and you won't have to call back to discuss the thing you forgot.

+ Have your spouse set the clocks forward an extra four minutes so you have a built-in cushion. Don't let them tell you when they do it.

+ Carry M&M's or Hershey Kisses in your purse for a quick chocolate fix for you, a reward for toddlers who use the big potty while you're out, or for a child who got a super grade on a test.

+ Small bottles of antibacterial hand sanitizers are great to have in the car when you have to eat a meal on the run.

+ Make an extra car-door key and put it in your wallet or diaper bag—so when your keys are dangling in the ignition of a locked car you won't have to panic!

+ Use milk crates turned on their sides for holding jeans, sweaters, and puzzles so little hands can reach them when needed.

+ Those double-tiered toy organizers are wonderful for corralling Barbies, Lincoln Logs, Legos, toy cars, small puzzles, and blocks. Type labels for each bin so kids know how to clean up; tape pictures of the item that goes in each bin for younger kids.

+ Use bread-wrap ties to loosely fold and secure long countertop appliance cords.

+ Place two or three extra trash bags at the bottom of the can. When you take out the trash, the next bag is right within your reach.

+ Buy different-colored bathroom towels and washcloths for each child. This ends the squabbling about whose is dirty and who didn't hang up their towel.

+ Do as much Christmas shopping as possible by catalog or Internet. Keep a list of what you buy so you don't duplicate a gift from year to year or forget what you have for someone.

+ Type and save addresses for Christmas cards on a disc. Keep track of those from whom you don't receive cards for two years; then streamline your list by considering dropping those names. Use the disc to print labels for addressing Christmas cards too.

+ Purchase an address stamp to save time writing out your address repeatedly on bills, invitations, or cards.

+ Send thank-you notes promptly. Help your children write their own too. Model gratitude for them. One mom shared this rule: "You can't wear/play with/read what you got until the thank-you note is written!"

+ Bathe small children who are close in age in assembly-line fashion.

+ Before washing, place baby and toddler socks in a mesh sweater bag, zip it, and toss the bag into the washer. This ends the hassle

of losing tiny socks on the backs of towels, in the insides of elas-
ticized sheets, and to the dryer monster.

+ Most lingerie and sweater items marked "hand wash only" can
be safely washed on the cool setting, delicate cycle. Zip them in
a mesh sweater bag and dry them on a sweater dryer (available
at any discount store).

+ Line cookie sheets with parchment paper for more even baking—
and so you don't have to scrub them when you're done. There
are even disposable Crock-Pot liners now.

Questions for Study and Reflection

1. Read Matthew 8:2, 12:44, and 23:25. What concept do each of
   these stories teach us about "cleanliness"?

2. The word *organize*, the way we would use it, isn't found in a Bible
   concordance. Does that mean God doesn't care about that aspect
   of our lives? What evidence (think stewardship, for starters) could
   suggest He would care about it?

3. OCD (obsessive-compulsive disorder) and excessive type A personality are very real problems. Christian women deal with them too.
   When can our desire to better our homes, selves, relationships, and
   schedules be wrong?

4. Read Hebrews 11:2. What were the "ancients" commended for?
   _____.

5. How does that play a part in our balance of order and living?

Action Plan

Choose one (yup, only one!) thing to cultivate as a worthy habit these next 21 days.

Journal

Write a prayer asking God to clean your heart, even as you bring order to your physical home.

Memorize

" A man with leprosy came and knelt before him and said, 'Lord, if you are willing, you can make me clean'" (Matthew 8:2).

Chapter 6

Taming the Type A Personality

We do not remember days,
we remember moments.

—Cesare Pavere

I think the quotation above might be true. I have very clear impressions of moments in my life. Every minute you have on this earth is the *chance* to make it a moment. A memory. I remember...

- the first time I felt each of my four children move inside my body.
- the joyous peal of my baby's belly laugh.
- the look in my husband's eyes when I said, "Yes. I'll marry you."
- the flash of candlelight on my wedding diamond the first night my husband and I spent the *whole* night together.
- the color of the waves the first time I ever saw the ocean.
- the first time I locked gazes with my newborns and saw recognition and pleasure dawn in their eyes.

* the love in my mother's eyes as she walked down the aisle as my matron of honor on my wedding day.

* my elation upon losing my first tooth.

* the day I stood on my sister's porch and cried as she made everything better without saying a word.

* the first time my daddy let go of my two-wheeler and I didn't fall over.

* the look on Emily's face when she delivers a spontaneous hug, running up and flinging herself against my knees.

* baby Elexa stopping me from finishing a lullaby, tiny hand across my mouth while she imitates me, whispering, "I yike that sweet nose, I yike that sweet mouth, I yove those sweet eyes..."

* the moment Eden learned to tie her shoes and I got teary-eyed while a gorgeous rainbow appeared in the sky.

* Ellie's utter exuberance as she bounds into my room each morning.

* the moment my college roommate and dear friend graduated and left for the real world—and the song that was playing while we packed and ate cold pizza.

* the clear, sparkly blue kindness of my daddy's eyes the last time I saw him.

* the slippery warmth of Baby Ellie's just-born body and the wail of her first cry.

* the patterned splash of the first tear that fell on my 56-years-young daddy's casket as I "showed" him my newest arrival; cancer took him 12 hours after her birth.

* the priceless, cute, and profound phrases I've heard from the lips of each of my children.

Why am I mentioning such moments at the beginning of a chapter about the type A personality? Because I am a recovering type A, and

I know what some of you are thinking. *What is wrong with this woman? This is supposed to be a book about loving and organizing your days in your home, as a mom, as a wife. I don't have much time here and I want the quick (preferably) ideas and organizational tips right now!*

Oh, precious girlfriends, I have been there, and I confess that I can still backslide. It is far too easy to miss out on the fullness of life as God intended it when we are caught up in a punishing, controlling, and fruitless quest for perfection. It would also be regrettably common to overlook the extraordinary in the often ordinary moments of our days.

Take this quick—I promise—quiz and test your propensity toward type A control. (Circle one choice for each statement.)

1. I am reluctant to delegate household tasks to others because I'm afraid that the work wouldn't be completed to my standards.	*True/False*
2. I have remade my child's bed because the sheets were rumpled/ the stuffed animals weren't straight/the comforter was crooked.	*True/False*
3. I have trouble relaxing when we entertain because I'm worried about the crumbs and the dirty dishes.	*True/False*
4. It's been a while since we've had company over because I'm waiting until the house is really clean.	*True/False*
5. I often either do not begin or do not complete projects because I know I won't be satisfied with the outcome.	*True/False*
6. When someone in my house sets down a glass or a coffee cup, I whisk it into the dishwasher immediately.	*True/False*
7. Relaxing is difficult or rare for me because productivity seems the richer choice.	*True/False*
8. I sometimes feel the way my children are dressed is a reflection on how good I am as a mother.	*True/False*
9. Feeling overwhelmed by my schedule or responsibilities often reduces me to tears.	*True/False*
10. I am a planner by nature. I like to have everything—company visits, vacations, dinner engagements, clipping the dog's toenails—on my calendar well in advance.	*True/False*

If you circled True for eight to ten questions, then this is the chapter for you! If you scored a True on five to seven questions, you might be a recovering perfectionist who has this battle partially under control. If you answered True on three to four questions, you are slowly losing the label "control freak." If you responded True to one or two questions, you're leaving your chains in the dust! Praise the Lord!

However, most of us, even the most happy-go-lucky kind of gals, harbor a small seed of perfectionism. There is something within us that makes us push, that causes us to doubt ourselves. It makes us prideful when we compare ourselves to others. Sometimes it causes us to feel inadequate without tangible things to show for our lives. Though perfectionism is not necessarily all bad. At its best, a perfectionist mind-set can goad us to achieve more than we ordinarily would. Type A tendencies motivate and inspire us to press on. At its worst, precious girlfriends, perfectionism is arrogance. It's the perverse streak in us that gets a thrill about reading the mildew regulations in Leviticus (*Leviticus*—the graveyard of Bible study, for crying out loud!). It allows us to mistakenly believe that we can do everything with excellence in our own power. That is a warped perspective and a heavy burden to carry.

"Cleanliness is not next to godliness. It isn't even in the same neighborhood. No one has ever gotten a religious experience out of removing burned-on cheese from the grill of the toaster oven."

Erma Bombeck

Let's consider some things God has to say about control, about perfection, about pride.

+ Romans 8:6: "The mind controlled by the Spirit is life and peace."
+ Galatians 5:22-23: "The fruit of the Spirit is...self-control."

- 2 Peter 1:6: "[Add] to knowledge, self-control."
- 1 Thessalonians 5:8: "Since we belong to the day, let us be self-controlled..."
- 2 Samuel 22:31,33: "As for God, his way is perfect;...[It is God who] makes my way perfect."
- Proverbs 18:12: "Before his downfall a man's heart is proud."
- Job 37:16: "[Do you know...] those wonders of him who is perfect in knowledge?"
- 1 John 4:18: "Perfect love drives out fear."
- Proverbs 8:13; 11:2; 29:23: "I hate pride and arrogance"; "When pride comes, then comes disgrace"; "A man's pride brings him low."
- Galatians 6:4: "Each one should test his own actions. Then he can take pride in himself, without comparing himself to somebody else."

Remember that the responsibility for having everything and everybody turn out perfectly is not yours. Not only is it not your responsibility, it's not even possible! Accidents happen. Dust bunnies reproduce. Milk spills. Parties flop. People have God-given free will, and they can and do exercise that will against our wishes or our best plans. Weather and children both have minds of their own.

Life is too short to save things for special occasions. After Linda's mother died, her friend, author Faith Andrews Bedford, helped her go through her mother's things. "Mother bought these linens when she and Dad went to Ireland 15 years ago," she said, running her fingers over the embroidery. "She never used them—said they were for a special occasion." Then Linda brought down a set of glasses purchased in Chicago that were to have been used to toast her mom and dad on their fiftieth wedding anniversary. Unfortunately, Linda's dad died after their forty-eighth. In her mother's upstairs closet Linda discovered a blue silk dress with sparkling rhinestone buttons. The tags were still attached.

Do you have any clothes you're saving for a vague occasion that might never arrive? Do you have "company" dishes and "family" dishes? Ever thought about why? Ever thought about vacuuming in taffeta if you feel like it? Set the table tonight with the very best for those you love best. I'm not saying that there aren't special things that need to be set up on a higher shelf or temporarily packed away. I am saying to lift the baby up high and gently allow his little fingers to touch the pretties you have. You can teach a healthy respect for precious things while letting him know there is nothing more precious than he is. And while I'm stepping on toes (mine included) might I suggest that if there is anything in your home too priceless to be looked at, enjoyed, touched, or used, that you give it to someone whose home is more suitable or reconsider your perspective.

Every week night while I was growing up, my daddy would have popcorn and watch Johnny Carson on *The Late Show*. One Christmas, I bought him a huge, creamy pottery bowl with writing that spelled out, Dad's Popcorn. Daddy went Home at the age of 56, just 12 hours after the birth of my third daughter. That popcorn bowl was one of the first things my mother gave to me. It is a testimony to how far I've come in my type A recovery that we use that bowl every single week on family night. I watch my little girls dipping sweet, child fists into that bowl, and I am flooded with memories and gratitude. If they ever do drop and break it, it still will have served its purpose. Besides, I think even such an accident would make Daddy laugh.

Perfectionism is linked to crankiness, and that leads to wrinkles! I wanted to throw something more lighthearted in this list because I know only too well how hard it is to relinquish control. How do you think I thought of all those quiz questions? Unfortunately, I didn't have to dig very far into my research. I am so pleasant when things go my way; I can be so edgy when things veer off the expected course. Have you been there? The relentless quest for something which is not possible, nor even approachable without God, causes discontent, envy, and stress.

Perfectionism burdens our marriages. Trust me, I know. For the first two days of our honeymoon, I wriggled out from under Greg's arm, and tiptoed to the bathroom to brush my hair and teeth and wash my face. I wanted him to think I woke up with sweet breath and lovely hair. By day three, I realized I had set an impossibly uncomfortable standard, and as I relaxed, the intimacy and trust blossomed between us. I have gotten a lot better, with some relapses.

A few years ago, I shared with my Sunday school class a conversation I had with my husband. I had been frustrated with what I saw as my recurrent inability to do anything right lately. I felt tired, cranky, wrung out, and done in. "What," my bewildered husband asked, "do you expect of yourself?"

I snuffled, wiping my nose on his T-shirt in a most attractive manner. "I, I," I hiccuped, "just want you to come home to a spotless house, for me to look marvelous and refreshed—with the children entertained, the meal hot, a great family evening prepared, my writing deadlines met—and to be available for incredible, mind-blowing sex any time you want!" He was incredulous. This wasn't at all what he expected of me. (However, he didn't voice any objections to my last proposal.) Greg is quite contented with me doing my best. "I'd rather come home to a happy wife than a spotless house," he told me. Why? He's a man. They're hopelessly realistic, and we're every bit as hopelessly idealistic. Maybe we need to get *real*.

"Perfect love casts out fear" (1 John 4:18). That doesn't mean a love with no mistakes in it, but a completing, mature love whose transparency only serves to reflect a greater love. Think of it, to be real enough to allow our husband to love us "as Christ loved the church" (Ephesians 5:25).

Perfectionism sets impossible standards for our children. As Erma Bombeck indicated in one of her columns, we don't want our wake-up call to be overhearing our children playing mommy to their dolls by reciting a list of schedules, claiming to be too busy to play. "Mommies don't act like that!" I often hear my girls bicker during their play, whenever one of them doesn't behave as they feel a grown-up mother should. I am usually quick to correct them. Yes, mommies play, mommies make mistakes, but hopefully our love makes up for many mistakes. The burden of perfectionism is not a trait we want to pass on to our children. Show them that mistakes can be profitable. When you're wrong, admit it. Ask their forgiveness if necessary. When you get lost on a trip, try and point out the beauty of an alternate route or the things you would have missed if you'd gone another way.

Perfectionism can cause us to miss out on God's best. By definition, perfectionism demands that we think we can do it alone. All by ourselves. Picture your two-year-old throwing an all-out tantrum. "*No!* Don't help me. *I can do it!*" It's like the old story of the traveling salesman who took his little girl to the toy store, wanting to purchase her a beautiful doll—an expensive, exquisite, porcelain creation, dressed in silk and carrying a parasol. But he told his daughter she could pick out any doll she wanted. She pushed away his suggestions with the refrain, "You said I could choose!" She picked out a cheap plastic baby doll. Within a week, that doll lay broken and abandoned in a corner of the closet. By insisting on her own way, she missed out on her father's best for her.

Recovery begins by relaxing your standards. Think of it. What's the worst that could happen if you made store-bought stuffing at Thanksgiving? Served company dinner on paper plates? Skipped dusting for a week? Two weeks? Betcha the world would keep on turning. Try it and see. I double-dog dare you.

"There is no pleasure in having nothing to do; the fun is in having lots to do and not doing it."

Mary Little

While I'm writing, a late January snow is beginning to dance elegantly, with flakes that are picking up speed and size. The view outside my office window is both lovely and cozy. My girls have noticed and are running around the house shrieking with glee. The oldest two are praying for a snow day tomorrow. I have just thrown miniature meatloaves in the oven for dinner, and I can smell the spicy-sweet brown sugar and mustard sauce wafting through the house. My desk is a mess, and I have so many more things I need to do. However, after further consideration, I can think of nothing more pressing than visiting the cozy disarray of each girl's room to giggle and read with them—and then snuggling in front of the fire with my husband who has, for the fourth time in history, come home twenty minutes early!

P.S.—We got the snow day!

Excuse This House

Some houses try to hide the fact
That children shelter there;
Ours boasts of it quite openly,
The signs are everywhere.
For smears are on the windows,
Little smudges on the doors;
I should apologize, I guess
For toys strewn on the floor.
But I sat down with the children
And we played and laughed and read,
And if the doorbell doesn't shine,
Their eyes will shine instead.
For when I have to choose between
The one job or the other,
Though I need to cook and clean,
First I'll be a
Mother.

—Unknown

QUESTIONS FOR STUDY AND REFLECTION

1. Look up the following scriptures and write down their common theme: Deuteronomy 32:4; 2 Samuel 22:31; Psalm 18:30; Hebrews 10:11. What is the only source of perfection?

2. Read Isaiah 26:3. How can we be kept in perfect peace?

3. Read Psalm 18:30,32. What is the relationship between God and our plans?

4. Read 2 Corinthians 7:1 and Hebrews 12:2. What do both verses see as a higher goal than perfection? Who perfects our faith?

5. Read Romans 12:2 and fill in the blanks. "Do not _____ any longer to the _____ of this _____, but be transformed by the renewing of your _____. Then you will be able to test and approve what God's will is—his _____, _____ and _____ will."

The world seems to say that business is a *form* of godliness. Don't you believe it! This verse reminds us not to accept worldly patterns of thought.

6. Is the pursuit of excellence necessarily a bad thing? Why or why not?

7. How did you do on the type A tendency test? (If you've already skipped ahead to the action plan, get back here—you've got it bad!) Read Hebrews 7:19. What does legalistic lawkeeping in pursuit of perfection gain us? If we know this, why do you suppose we still strive for an unattainable goal?

8. Look at Romans 12:2 again. Do you ever have difficulty believing

that God's will for your life is perfect? If so, memorize Jeremiah 29:11.

Action Plan

Think it through: If you don't finish five items on your to-do list, or you take a store-bought dish to the potluck dinner, what would be the worst that could happen? This week, take your to-do list in your hand with you when you pray. Ask God to help you accomplish your tasks, be productive, and to open your eyes to priorities and opportunities that might be even more important than your list. As I was working on a writing deadline this week, I got a call asking me to play the piano at a funeral. I felt so much like declining. I only had four days left in which to meet that deadline. But then I reconsidered. I could not write "People are more important than things" without living it. I played for that funeral, trusting that God will bless right choices. And He always does. Always. Cling to that.

Journal

Write a prayer to God confessing your need for control and your desire to relinquish that control to Him. Please really spend some time on this, and if you don't feel ready to give up control yet, to quote Beth Moore, then pray for a "willingness to be willing." Ask God to give you a discerning heart about where your stated priorities and daily actions don't match.

Memorize

"I, wisdom, dwell together with prudence; I possess knowledge and discretion" (Proverbs 8:12).

Chapter 7

Choosy Mothers Choose Jif— Real Mothers Buy Generic

Daddy! The smoke alarm went off,
so mommy must be ready for us to eat!

—*The Dagnan Children*

No doubt if you're considering the option of staying home, or have already committed to it, you're finding that financially, things are a bit tight. (Okay, that's enthusiastically euphemistic for downright scary!) It helps to prepare yourself and your family, both practically and emotionally.

Getting Ready

Preparing Your Children

If you have preschool or early-elementary-aged children, include them in your discussions. They'll probably be thrilled at the thought of having you more available to them; however, explain that there will be some trade-offs. You may get to be a room mother or a volunteer at their school, but dinners out and the little extras they're accustomed to on shopping trips will be curtailed.

"I think of our family table as a training ground
for all of life, a place where adults and children
alike can learn to put aside their differences
in favor of laughter and fellowship."

Katrina Kenison

Older children may not seem as outwardly excited, but I know from many discussions with my high school students that most of them appreciated the mothers who stayed home. In a survey I did of two year's worth of sociology classes, a whopping 81 percent of female students remarked either that they wished their mothers had stayed home or that they were planning to stay home when they became mothers themselves. It is interesting to note that 73 percent of my male students also stated that they would like for their future wives to be able to stay home at least until the children were in school. Although older children are certainly more independent, they need you for different things and perhaps need you even more when they reach the pressures and challenges of middle school and high school.

Preparing Yourself

+ *Practice living on just one income as soon as possible before you quit.* Instead of reaching for the phone to order pizza or carry-out, try soup and sandwiches or a cookout on the grill. Put all you can in a savings account.

+ *Write down all existing debt.* Begin reducing credit cards by paying off the smallest balance first. Then combine that payment with the minimum payment of another card until that's paid off, then on to the next one, and so forth.

+ *Check out a debt-consolidation loan.* If you've fallen into the nasty credit trap known as immediate gratification, a consolidation loan can greatly reduce both interest and monthly expenses.

+ *Consider selling one car if you own two.* Or if it is a necessity to have two cars, buy an older, affordable one for errands around town or try to pay off one car completely before you quit work.

+ *Make a list of all of your fixed monthly expenditures.* Highlight anything which could be eliminated. In particular pay attention to newspaper and magazine subscriptions, bottled water services, and cable television.

+ *Arrange work schedules.* Several mothers, at least for a season, mentioned that they and their husband worked opposing shifts—he during the day and she at night. That way there were no child-care expenses and the children were always with one parent. However, this is tough on a marriage; it isn't a great long-term solution.

+ *Research options for flextime,* working at home, or caring for other children in your home.

+ *Keep giving.* Tempting though it is, don't skip tithing when finances grow tight and bills mount. God honors such faithfulness, and your faithfulness sets a great example for your children.

+ *Be creative.* Talk with other mothers at home; brainstorm together creative ideas for conserving limited resources.

Tips, Ideas, and Hints

Practical Suggestions

+ *Add up that loose change.* We have a container that we affectionately call the "Happy Box." That way we always have quick milk money, school treat-day money, car-wash quarters, and miscellaneous savings. When the Happy Box is full, we might enjoy a movie or splurge on a pizza. Get over how it feels to pay with rolls of change!

+ *Start a Christmas club at your bank.* Most of these accounts only require $5 to open. They hold your money until late October or early November, then they issue a check for the amount you've saved. One of our tricks is to round off any paychecks or unexpected funds we receive. For example, if a check is for $278.72, we put $8.72 into Christmas club and the remainder in our checking account. We usually end up with $300 to $400 saved for holiday shopping. Between purchasing gifts throughout the year and having Christmas club money for late shopping, we almost always have a Christmas without adding to our debt.

+ *Shop at garage sales and consignment shops* for really good deals on kids' clothing and any furniture you might need. Shopping on eBay can be a fun option too. Sears has a Kidvantage program where they replace any item that wears out before your child outgrows it!

+ *Swap clothes with a friend who wears the same size.* When you've accumulated a pile of clothes that you're tired of wearing, pass hand-me-downs back and forth for children who are close in age.

Shopping Tips

+ *Buy generic or store-brand items whenever possible.* I've noticed that for most things, it doesn't make a big difference in taste or quality. This is particularly true of paper goods, dog food, and soups for cooking. Some of the off-brands of lotions, baby care items, and shampoos are wonderful. In my opinion, Luvs have the best leak protection for the best price (I know, I sound like a commercial, but I really *have* tried them all!). However, my sister and I both agree that Cheerios have to be real Cheerios, and Oreos must be the real deal too. While you're at it, make it DoubleStuff.

+ *Clip and use coupons wisely.* Use only the ones for items you would normally buy or to try a new item that you've actually been wanting to try. My girls love a certain breakfast cereal that they know they get only when we have a coupon.

+ *Take advantage of rebates and rain checks.* These can be surprisingly good deals. For their anniversary year, Office Max put out a flyer of rebates, including items that were free (except for tax) after the mail-in rebate. We've mailed in rebate offers for everything from bras to cookies.

+ *Buy items like toilet paper, paper towels, diapers, and soap in bulk* at discount warehouses. Sometimes Sam's Club and Costco will offer free one-day or one-week trial memberships. Take advantage of those in order to check out whether or not membership dues are worth it for your family. At any grocery store, make sure to check the unit price; bigger is not always cheaper.

+ *Discount grocery chains can be great for stocking up* on canned goods and other items. Other moms I've talked to love the day-old bakery stores for bread and lunch box goodies.

+ *Plan your menu around the grocery-store flyers* and then make your list from the menu. Some stores will honor ad matches too.

+ *Don't go to the grocery store without a list.* I have a magnetic paper pad on my refrigerator. Members of my family who are old enough to do so are responsible for writing down items that they use the last of. Double-check any recipes you're using so that you won't have to make last minute runs to the grocery store for missing ingredients. I have a master grocery list that makes planning a snap. I am refining one that goes in the order of our local Wal-Mart store (see...type A). I make copies of the master list on pretty pastel papers and keep some in a file. To make shopping more fun for (and thus easier with) the children, try providing school-age kids with a calculator. Let them add up the prices of everything you're putting into the cart to make sure you're staying on budget. Let preschoolers help place items in the cart. For in-the-cart toddlers, laminate pictures of items you need (pictures of brand name items are easy to find in magazines and newspaper grocery flyer sections), punch holes in the tops and place on an oversize clip ring or tie with a piece of yarn for a grocery necklace. Let the kids take turns choosing certain items. For example: This week Eden gets to pick the cereal, Emmy the Pop-Tarts, Ellie the lunch-box snacks, and Elexa the kind of cheese.

+ *On all purchases, and not just at the grocery store, avoid impulse spending.* List-making curtails this. So does leaving charge cards at home. (Putting them in ice does *not* work. You'll only electrocute yourself trying to melt them with the blowdryer the day of a big sale.) Try not to buy the item you want for at least 24 hours. If you leave without the item, often it will be too much work to return, and you won't buy it. Make a pact with your spouse that neither one of you will buy an item costing more than $50 (or whatever works with your budget) without discussing it with each other.

Now That You Have Groceries...

"There is no spectacle on earth more appealing than that of a beautiful woman in the act of cooking dinner for someone she loves."

Thomas Wolfe

Hands down, one of my least favorite questions is "What's for dinner?" While I am a good baker, I am not a good cook—and frankly, I don't really like to do it. Ask my husband about the crunchy baked beans…I mean, really, who knew you had to cook them first! In fact, before the advent of children, I saw no problem with using a not-insignificant portion of my grocery budget to put really wonderful clothes on layaway! Sigh. There's a world of difference between my husband's idea of what constitutes a necessity and my own ideas.

You may be a wonderful cook, or like me, just a bit culinary-impaired. Either way, I have found some great tips, recipes, and plain-old shortcuts for making the whole dinner preparation thing more palatable. (For recipes and menu-planning ideas, see Mom Aid #2.)

Dining Is a Family Event

If you have children old enough to make decisions, let them choose one entrée for each week. While this leads to a somewhat predictable diet of macaroni and cheese, hot dogs, or peanut butter and jelly, the children will appreciate giving their input. If your children are in junior or senior high, assign them one night a week or several nights a month to prepare dinner. This is wonderful training and a great help too. Delegate one night to your spouse and one additional night for soups or sandwiches to make a tough job easier.

Growing up, we always had pizza from whichever pizza parlor we had a coupon for on Thursday nights. It was my mother's standing beauty shop appointment night and my dad's night to cook. These pizza dates were great treats and became a memorable tradition.

One family gets together with good friends every Friday night and they either chip in for pizza, have sandwiches, or pool their leftovers. They watch a family-friendly movie and have a fun time of fellowship.

One family budgets for eating out one night a week; they take turns choosing the place. In our family, we sometimes put names of possible restaurants on slips of paper and into a bowl. The children take turns drawing, and no one is allowed to complain.

Quick Tips

However, as much as we might wish, eating out is not always an option. And it can be a budget-buster. So what to do? Well, there are several books out about once-a-month cooking. I've heard this is ideal, especially if you have a large deep freeze. Frankly that concept overwhelms me, but if you can do this, more power to you! However, for the rest of us slackers, I do have some easier ideas that I've actually managed to incorporate into my routine.

- Brown a week's worth of ground beef and refrigerate recipe portions in Tupperware containers or freeze in small freezer bags. Then when you get ready to make pizza, spaghetti, tacos, or casseroles, the hard work is already done. If you are making something like lasagna that freezes well, use two 9 x 13 pans and double the batch. You'll have dinner for tonight and one for later as well. Do the same with cookie dough and bread dough. If you freeze the dough in little balls, you'll have convenient, hot homemade cookies or rolls without the expense of store-bought dough. Bottom line: As long as you're making a mess anyway, make it a *big*, productive one!

- Find another mom who likes to cook and when you double your casserole recipe, trade one or several of your hot dishes for some of hers. You'll both get several meals and get to try out some new things as well. My neighbor and I did this for a few weeks after she proofread this chapter. It was awesome! We still trade off baking goodies for one another.

- Our Moms Night Out group—tired of having the same old thing for dinner—got together and exchanged recipes. Our only criteria was that they had to be easy to make, include ingredients we'd probably already have on hand (no weird, unpronounceable spices), and have been previously approved by actual children.

+ One mother, Marla, shared with me that when she tries a new recipe she has her family rate it. If they really enjoy it and want her to fix it again, she marks it with a red star. That saves time when rifling through the recipe box and wondering if anyone will eat it!

+ Don't overlook the grill and the Crock-Pot as great time-savers. Throw in a pot roast with cream of mushroom soup, a packet of dried onion soup mix, potatoes, yellow onion, and carrots. Turn it on low at night before bed for the next day's lunch or that morning for the evening's supper. It's wonderful to have dinner waiting at the end of the day. Marinate stew meat in Italian dressing to tenderize and flavor the meat for grilled shish kebabs.

+ Try planning a month's worth of seasonal menus. That way you can recycle four menus that will be rotated every three months. During less busy weeks, I try to introduce one new recipe, just to keep meals from becoming boring. For spring include barbecued brisket and brown sugar ham; for summer, veggie pizzas and anything grilled outside; for autumn, spicy chili and pasta casseroles; for winter, thick stews and Mexican casseroles. Use one of those free spiral bound planner calendars that businesses hand out or purchase an inexpensive one at an office supply store. Once a week, before you go grocery shopping, write out your menu in the block for each day. Be sure to include any meals out both in your planner and on the menu.

+ Paste recipes you've clipped from magazines onto 8 ½ x 11 sheets of paper, slip them into plastic protector sheets and place them in a three-ring binder for easier access.

+ Open that cookbook you've been wanting to try. Leaf through it, and mark twelve new recipes that appeal to you. Try making a new one each month, and let your family be the cook-off judges.

Taste of Home magazine, *Gooseberry Patch,* and *Pampered Chef* cookbooks are all excellent, realistic sources of yummy new food.

- When you're cooking, clean up as you go. In fact, apply this principle to everything in your home. It will greatly simplify the amount of big cleaning jobs that you have to do. My family is pretty well trained about this and spoiled by me. Only this morning my husband commented, "I can tell we're on deadline, it's the only time the house looks like this. I think it just makes us appreciate you more."

Dining Out

1. If you have really young children, begin by playing restaurant at home and practicing manners.

2. Decide ahead of time how to keep costs to a minimum. For example, only order water to drink and avoid desserts and side dishes that don't accompany the meal.

3. Check out the specials that various restaurants offer. Some chains allow one child under four to eat free for each paying adult. Others offer special pricing on buffets according to age. We ate at one nice restaurant three times in one month because they were running a special— if you saved your receipt and could compare it to another restaurant's similar meals, the meal would be half-price! Try pizza places for certain nights when kids eat free.

4. Check the Internet for coupons to your favorite establishment.

5. Some cities have Entertainment coupon books that function like dinner clubs, with 50 percent off or buy-one-get-one free offers, for a nominal fee. Also check school fund-raisers for similar deals at local fast food establishments.

Dining In

As I'm sure you know, keeping little ones interested at the dinner table can be a chore; as they get older, the challenge becomes how to engage them in conversation. At our house, we follow a loose (really loose) schedule of dinner table activity. (By the way, be sure to acknowledge kids' food stages without making them too big a deal. It's also a great idea to allow every kid two foods that they don't have to eat if they don't like them. Make gathering around the table a fun place to be.)

Monday—book night. Since Mondays are our library days, each family member gets to bring the book they are reading with them to the table. We read as we eat and perhaps share a little about what we're reading or a fun quote or scene from the book. I know it's breaking table etiquette to read at the table, but it's building memories and encouraging a lifelong love of reading.

Tuesday and Thursday—table talk. We started having these planned discussions after I found a delightful resource published by Focus on the Family—*Table Talk: Easy Activity and Recipe Ideas for Bringing Your Family Closer at Mealtime* by Mimi Wilson and Mary Beth Lagerborg (Focus on the Family Publishing, 1994). We occasionally use some of their ideas, and at other times, some of our own. I put our questions for table talk on colored index cards and let the children draw one or two. We don't usually vary from this routine, even with company over. In fact, it's a great way to put guests at ease and have a surefire conversation starter.

Examples to get you talking at the table:

+ What color was your day?
+ Tell about the funniest thing that happened to you today.
+ What is your favorite scripture verse or Bible story? Why?

+ If you could have dinner with any famous person, who would it be and why?

+ If you were going to interview a president (past or present) or a celebrity and could only ask three questions, what would they be?

+ What is your favorite family memory?

+ Mom and Dad—share the story of how you asked your spouse/ were asked by your spouse to be married.

+ If our family received a huge inheritance, what three things would you buy for our family? What three things would you buy for someone else? What three charities would you donate money to?

+ Where would you like to go on vacation?

+ If time travel were possible, when in history or the future would you go?

+ What things make you grumpiest? Happiest?

+ What is it about your favorite teacher that makes him or her your favorite teacher?

+ What subject do you like best in school? Least?

+ What is your favorite season? What's your favorite tradition and special food during that season?

+ If you could have a guest to our home this month, whom would you choose?

+ What one thing have we never done as a family that you wish we'd do?

+ Go around the table and share two things you like about every person here.

+ What do you think about guardian angels?

+ What worries you most? Of what are you most proud?

Wednesday and Friday—family devotions. These are short ones, very different from our family night or occasional nighttime devotions. Two of our favorite books are: *What Would You Do If ?...101 Five-Minute Devotions for the Family* by Greg Johnson (Servant Publications, 1995) and *The One Year Book of Devotions for Girls* edited by Debbie Bible and Betty Free (Tyndale House, 2000). They have one for boys too. Sometimes, we use *Little Visits With God* and *More Little Visits with God* by Allan Jahsmann (Concordia Publishing House)—these are the ones my parents used with us.

Saturday—free day. On rare occasions, we will eat in front of the television for a family movie night.

Sunday—family night. Get a chalkboard marquee for announcing the menu and activities—it builds anticipation. Here are a few ideas to entice you (we'll explore more ideas later in the book):

+ Incorporate variety. Perhaps close your meal with prayer rather than praying before the meal.

+ Have a backwards night, with your clothes facing backward and serve dessert first.

+ Let the children help prepare certain meals.

+ To help children learn to set the table, get different sheets of colored construction paper (one for each member of your family) and trace the shapes of a plate, cup, fork, knife, spoon, and napkin in their proper places. Or, cut out pictures of those items from magazines. Then laminate the sheets to use as placemats and a handy guide for table setting!

+ If you live out of the city limits, cook hot dogs and s'mores around a campfire.

+ Grill and dine outside, complete with tablecloth and fresh flowers.

+ Light candles on the table. Play dinner music.

Whatever you choose to do, just try to eat dinner together at least four times a week and at least one meal a day as a family.

When they are presented and planned with love and care, family meals can be more than just food for the body. They can be soul food—a form of family worship.

The table is really the family altar!
Here those of all ages come together and help sustain
both their physical and their spiritual existence.
…A family meal
can be a sacrament.
It entwines the material and the spiritual in a remarkable way.
…Here, at one common table
is the father who has earned,
the mother
who has prepared or planned,
and the children who share according to need,
whatever their antecedent participation may have been.
…We can understand something of why our Lord, when he broke bread
with his little company toward the end of their earthly fellowship,
told them, as often as they did it, to remember him.
…There is no reason why each family meal should not take
on something of the character of a time of memory and hope.
—Elton Trueblood

"At feasts, remember that you are entertaining
two guests: body and soul. What you give
to the body, you presently lose; what you
give to the soul, you keep forever."

Epictetus

Questions for Study and Reflection

1. Why is sharing a meal with someone an intimate thing to do?

2. Even the disciples and Jesus' hosts learned lessons at the "table." Check out Luke 7:36-43; 9:11-17; 14:1-14; 22:27. What lessons can you teach your children and learn from your children at the table?

3. Have other group members share about what factors make a meal memorable to them.

4. Read the wonderful story in John 21:1-14. Why do you think Jesus chose mealtime to reveal Himself a third time to the disciples after His resurrection?

5. Read Proverbs 15:17. Has there ever been a family meal in which sour dispositions, harsh words, or heavy sighs has ruined appetites? Which family member generally sets the table mood? What steps can you take to ensure that mealtimes are pleasant ones?

6. Initiate a conversation with someone in your Bible study, neighborhood, or circle of friends whose mealtimes you admire. Ask them to share "secrets" of making this precious time one of delight, rather than stress. Record some ideas here.

Action Plan

+ Play music during your meal.

+ Try one new recipe this week.

+ Actively plan an activity to accompany a meal this week. A simple devotion or a few table talk starters would be a great place to begin.

Journal

Write about the most special childhood meal of which you've ever been a part. Was it a wedding feast? A birthday party? Your grandparents' anniversary celebration? A special picnic? Describe the people who were present. Relive the atmosphere. Revive the tastes, sounds, and sights in your memory and transfer them to paper.

Memorize

"Better a meal of vegetables where there is love than a fattened calf with hatred" (Proverbs 15:17).

Chapter 8

It's Mommy Time!

*Ah! There is nothing like staying
home for real comfort.*

—Jane Austen

I was experiencing a rare moment of bliss. I swayed gently on our porch swing, a two-year-old sang "Jesus Loves Me," a sweet baby gurgled in a bouncy seat at my feet, and my seven-year-old "cooked" soup at her play kitchen. And you know something? I was cheating. I read snatches of a current magazine while occasionally looking up to admire a creation, clap for an impromptu concert, smile with a full heart at the baby, or taste a culinary delight. Yep, I was having mommy time of sorts, straddling the fence between childhood and my former grown-up life.

One of the best secrets of successful stay-at-home moms (or any mom for that matter) is the cultivation of mommy time. Perhaps nothing is so important or so illusive to mothers as relaxation time undisturbed by glass shattering, phones ringing, or anything requiring a trip to the emergency room.

So why exactly is this so hard to come by? Because we are genetically and environmentally predisposed to be nurturers. And we're good at it. We want to be wonderful wives, dedicated mothers, compassionate girl-friends, competent employees, perky volunteers, informed citizens, and talented mentors. I'm exhausted just making the list! We dedicate the bulk of our days to the needs of others. If we squeeze out any extra time, we feel like we should give it to our spouses so that we still *have* a rela-tionship after the children grow up, putting us out of a job.

And that, girlfriends, leaves us exactly 11 minutes of alone time from 10:49 PM to 11:00 PM before we fall asleep with that nagging list of *things to do tomorrow* still swirling around our heads.

All mommies, working or not, have bought into the myth that carv-ing out time to do something we want to do is selfish, neglectful, or both. I've noted that men do not have this problem, and they are healthier for its lack. My husband is one of the hardest working men I know, but when he is done, he simply says, "Enough," and lounges in the daddy chair. He does absolutely nothing and is completely fine with that. Guilt free! Although, as one author put it, on several occasions when I've followed his example, some of our children were conceived.

At the risk of borrowing from a L'Oreal or McDonald's advertise-ment, you *are* worth it and you *do* deserve a break today. We need a break because often, even during family fun times, we constantly feel on duty. We're the family lookout, buffer, caretaker, and organizer. We monitor fights, cut up food, and blow on french fries. And to top it all off, the guilt we feel if we've chosen to stay home multiplies because we don't divide chores, delegate responsibilities, or ask for things too often. After all, we're home now. We need to do everything, all by ourselves, from scratch and without an ounce of help from anybody.

Involve your husband in actively raising your children. You benefit, he benefits, and the children benefit. So what if he doesn't wash their hair, fold the clothes, apply a Band-Aid, or dust like you do? It's help, so don't knock it. If we feel solely responsible for every nurturing role in the family, we get overloaded and make ourselves vulnerable to depression and to a sense of self-defeat. It is not worth it.

So, hopefully now you're convinced of the need for and benefits of mommy time. Sit back with a pencil, your dreams, a diet vanilla Coke, and a small handful of chocolate-covered potato chips, and let your imagination go wild!

What Counts as Mommy Time?

Anything you enjoy doing that does not involve the children's immediate needs.

Window shopping. Antiques browsing. Novel reading. Making something creative. (Party favors for the entire fourth grade do *not* count!)

Naps count only if they're taken for fun—not if you're trying to take one to recoup from last night's refreshing three hours of sleep when all the kids were up with croup/ear infections/thunderstorm phobia/bad dreams.

Going out with "just the girls!" About every eight weeks I meet with a group of girlfriends for an early dinner (cheaper menu prices) or a movie. Meet a friend for lunch or share a dessert. For five years some friends and I indulged in an annual autumn getaway. One night filled with cobblestone streets of antiques, craft shops, and bakeries, giggles, too many calories, wild hairdo experimentation, facials, and manicures. I always returned home ready to roll after this time of fellowship.

Ideas for Mommy Time

Plan it. It will *never* just happen.

Give yourself time. If you have really young children, use the timer for more than time out. Set it for 10-15 minutes and announce: "When the timer goes beep, beep, beep, then Mommy will read you a story. But right now I need you to play quietly. When I'm done with my time, I will be a much better Mommy." When Emmy was two, I overheard her doing this with her dolls while leafing through one of my magazines!

It's okay to take time in spurts. A ten-minute bath here, a chapter of a book there, a swiped chocolate-covered strawberry you've been hiding in the back of the fridge.

Take up a hobby. Sewing. Cross-stitching. Scrapbooking (okay, that might border on an obsession). Gardening. Painting. Riding horseback. Gourmet cooking. Sketching. I like to cross-stitch. It's easy, and it's something I can do to relax even when I can't get away or if we're all watching a movie together or the kids are making big-time noise.

Sit still and do absolutely nothing. Daydream. Reflect. Catnap. Most of us feel that if we have an idle moment, we should be doing something. Most women I talk to are just like me. If they ever did watch a television show, they had a moral compunction to hop up on every commercial break to do laundry, fold clothes, do a few dishes, or at least serve snacks to the rest of the family. But even God rested (remember that Sabbath thing?) and even dirt needs rest—every seven years the land needs to lie fallow. Seems to me like that's good enough evidence that we need rest too.

Take a nap. The average child's nap time that I got from polling mothers was two hours. It is well worth the effort to coordinate their schedules. Children around kindergarten age who no longer take naps can have what my ingenious sister calls QT (quiet time). Often they'll fall asleep anyway, but they're not so offended by the idea that they might still need naps. It is my strong suggestion, especially if you have an infant or preschooler, that *you* sleep for the first 45 minutes. New research is finding that a 45- to 90-minute nap during the middle of the day can be as refreshing to your mind and body as a full night's sleep. Not only will you have more energy, but by napping first, you don't run the risk of being sidetracked by doing just one more thing and using up all your time or having the children wake up early.

Be a friend. Cultivating and maintaining friends is hard work, but so worth the payoff. Women embrace the concept that joy shared is doubled and sorrow shared is halved. Friendship is a wise investment. You may not even realize this until you really need a friend. Have another friend with small children come over to help you houseclean. Turn up the jammin' music, give the children one room to trash, and clean like crazy. Reward yourselves with a chocolate treat. Then go to her house and do the same on another day. Swap two-hour blocks of time in which you can run errands alone or escape.

Take the children to the park. Bring along a magazine for yourself. Books don't work here, but magazines are great because you can read short articles in between choruses of "Mommy, watch me!" "Mommy, push me!" "Can you slide too?"

Read poetry. It sounds silly, but it's so relaxing. Read the chapter of Proverbs that corresponds with the day of the month. Go to the Psalms. Read Robert Frost, Emily Dickinson, Yeats, Tennyson, Wordsworth, the Brownings.

Dream. Have a long-term goal to dream about and work toward. One mother I talked to is just now going back to college. "I wish people wouldn't ask me what degree I want. I don't know. I only know that I've spent so long at home that I just feel dumb. This is my time now." I'm so glad she's taking it. If that time seems far off to you, trust me, it isn't. My own precious girls have just turned 4, 7, 9 and 15. I know that I will blink again and they'll be gone. But until then it helps to dream. Get a decorating book or a book of house plans. Subscribe to a professional magazine that helps keep you updated on your former life. Take an extension or Internet class. Sign up for a crafts class or technology class at a junior college.

Rock the baby for an extra ten minutes after he's asleep. Oh, I know, there are a hundred other things you could be doing. But for these short minutes, bow your head on his fuzzy one. Plant kisses in his hair. Whisper of your love for him in those perfect seashell ears. Close your eyes, breathe in that sweet baby smell, and say a prayer of thanks.

Rediscover candlelight. Put some on the table at dinner. I do this, even with small children. Light one in your bedroom. Each night at dusk, I light candles. Their shadows dance on the walls and the fragrance fills our home. The girls have gotten so used to this ritual, they often follow me around and then beg to be the one who blows them out again at bedtime.

Enjoy the decadent pleasure of preparing your own lunch after feeding the children theirs, and read a good book as you eat.

Make a corner of the family room or your bedroom a haven just for you. Fill it with things that relax, refresh, and restore you. Browse through old photo albums and yearbooks and reminisce in this space.

One of the most liberating epiphanies is to acknowledge that your work will never be done. Dirty laundry can procreate faster than you can read one Mother Goose rhyme. But you can't reclaim these moments, these days. Make the most of each one.

Eleven Stress Busters to Help You Enjoy Mommy Time

1. Breathe deeply. Count to ten and decide if whatever it is you're worrying about is something you can solve. If it is, quit stressing and make a plan of action. If it isn't, turn it over to God.

2. Remember that for every minute you spend unwinding, you'll probably gain ten in productivity.

3. Chronic stress makes you look, act, and feel old. It steals energy, hours of sleep, and is even connected to weight gain and a host of other more serious things.

4. Live in the moment.

5. Go outside and gulp fresh air.

6. Walk whenever possible.

7. Listen to a variety of music.

8. Garbage in, garbage out. What is it that you read, watch, dwell on? Could your mind use some weeding?

9. Relax your standards. Skip dusting this week. Let the old sheets stay on the bed one more day. Send store-bought cookies to school this time.

10. Put in your favorite tape or CD. If you have a fireplace or porch swing, sit there and drink cocoa, coffee, or tea.

11. Rock on the front porch in the rain.

Busy with the Right Things

In his insightful little book *Home with a Heart*, Dr. James Dobson shares his perception of the biggest threat facing the American family today. The answer is not what you might think. "It is the simple matter of overcommitment and the tyranny of the urgent."

Chronic busyness all too often equals stress. Remember, that adds up to wrinkles, destroyed sleep patterns, and a litany of other health problems—from cancer to heart disease. Does that describe your lifestyle even though you're at home? If so, rethink your priorities. Did you stay home so you could keep a perfect house or did

you stay home so you could be the best wife
and mother possible? It might mean you have
to let go. That means if you've already made a
furious cleaning sweep through the house and
you find the lost checker and you're too tired to
put it back in the bag, throw it in the bottom of
the fruit bowl. It won't make a bit of difference,
I promise.

The Gifts of Books and Friends

One of the most fun things I have ever done while reclaiming my
mommy time was to form a book club. I had heard about them, wished
someone would invite me to join theirs, lamented the lack of my involvement in one, and then quit whining and just decided to start my own.
Whenever I speak to mothers, these are by far some of the most frequently
asked questions about mommy time—*How did you start the book club?
What do you read? How do you decide what to read? How often do you
meet? What's the format?* I'll do my best to answer all those questions with
our story, but if you have other questions or want to share a neat story or
suggestion from your own book club, please e-mail me!

Two months before we began the book club in January, I mailed fancy
tea party invitations to 15 women. Some of them I knew well; others I
just knew liked to read. I specified two things for that first meeting: 1)
this is a child-free get-together, and 2) everyone needs to bring a list of
five potential books from a variety of categories. Although Sharris, Vickie,
Patty, Lori, Karen, and Lindsay still make fun of me for the overly dainty
(okay, they called them shot glasses) tea cups, we had a ball bantering and
debating over the final book selections, giggling, and munching on sandwiches and other treats.

We agreed to meet for five months, taking the month of December off
since the season is too busy. We chose to read books in five categories:

- 2 classics—which we define as those books you were supposed to read in high school but didn't.

- 1 biography.

- 3 secular works—novels, current best-sellers.

- 3 inspirational books—usually Christian fiction, although we have also read from Jan Karon's Mitford series (and twice they have voted to read my books).

- 1 self-improvement book—marriage, family, parenting, organization.

And 1 selection is left open for lobbying.

Our first year involved a process of learning what we did and did not like. We have since then refined our guidelines and added some rules. We meet one Monday night a month from 6:30 to 8:30 PM. We rotate hosting and being responsible for discussion questions. The hostess is responsible for dinner or snacks (her choice) which coordinate with that month's book. Food may be something specifically mentioned in the book or merely something that fits with the book's era or theme. Because our very first hostess, Sharris, was so stunning, we have also kept the tradition of sending each member away with a small, inexpensive favor, also related to the book. We have agreed that hostess duties and discussion duties can never overlap.

Examples of Our Selections

Since I am always asked for examples, I'll share some here. Sharris hosted our meeting to discuss *The Scarlet Letter*. She served fresh veggies and dip, cheese and crackers, and huge sugar cookies with a letter A piped on them in red frosting. At evening's end we each took home a red rose with a quote from the book printed on an elegant white card tied to it with red ribbon. Lori gave everyone a set of delicate windchimes, an item taken from a pivotal scene in *Redeeming Love*. Vickie served scrumptious taco salad from baked tortilla bowls since the Bush family eats lots of Tex-Mex, as we learned in *George and Laura*.

Some current books have book club or reading guides in the back. We have also found discussion questions from the Internet, Cliff's Notes, and our own reading. We have laughed, cried, and probed, using the questions as a springboard for soul-searching and relationship building. And although we haven't enjoyed all books equally, they have broadened our horizons, taken us out of our comfort zones, and challenged intellects that we had thought were lost beneath a jumble of toys and endless cracker crumbs.

Other Ideas

Several on our original list of invitees loved the idea of a book club but were overcommitted at that time, or for some reason couldn't participate. I was disappointed, but since those faltering initial meetings, the group has become far more than a book club; we have bared our souls and bonded beyond our wildest expectations. For that reason, we decided to close membership for now. However, at the beginning of each selection period, we discuss whether or not current members would like others to join. You might want to invite new members at the beginning of your annual selection period, or you may choose to leave yours open year round. The fun of this is that there isn't a right or wrong way to do it.

Other things that we have found helpful: we have agreed that our meetings are for grown-ups only. Children who can crawl and go longer than two hours between feedings cannot attend book club night. If for some reason one of us cannot finish the book for that month, they cannot participate in the discussion part of the evening. During our free month we get together at a grown-up restaurant and come prepared to select the next year's reading list. Each member brings suggestions (the actual book or a review or advertisement is preferred) for books in at least three categories. Then each one gets a chance to lobby for one particular book.

We narrow down the selections to four in each category and then vote for three out of the four. This process usually works fairly well, however, we're flexible. For example, one year, we had so many in our inspirational category that we chose to forego the usual number of classics.

We've developed such a bond that next year for my fortieth birthday we are taking a book club trip together. We've accomplished this trip goal by charging book club dues of $10.00 per month. Each month's take is deposited into a savings account so that our August book can be read on a beach somewhere in Texas. After paying for accommodations and gasoline, the rest of the money will be divided among us for food and souvenirs.

All seven of us together, alone. Yep, no husbands and no kids for a long weekend. A road trip, late night giggles, abundant junk food, facials, lounging. Ahhhh. There are rumors of club getaways every two years. I'll keep you posted. Meanwhile, here are four years of our book selections. I hope they inspire you to connect with great women and great reads.

Sample Book Club List #1	
January	*The Scarlet Letter*, Nathaniel Hawthorne
February	*Redeeming Love*, Francine Rivers
March	*The Notebook*, Nicholas Sparks
April	*Rebecca*, Daphne du Maurier
May	*The Strand*, Ellen Vaughn
June	*A Painted House*, John Grisham
July	*Finding the Hero in Your Husband*, Julianna Slattery
August	*Theory of Relativity*, Jacquelyn Mitchard
September	*Wuthering Heights*, Emily Brontë
October	*The Lights of Home*, Cindy Sigler Dagnan
November	*At Home in Mitford*, Jan Karon
December	Ornament exchange and book selection for upcoming year

Sample Book Club List #2	
January	*Mrs. De Winter* (sequel to *Rebecca*), Susan Hill
February	*Making Sense of the Men in Your Life*, Kevin Leman
March	*A Light in the Window*, Jan Karon
April	*George and Laura*, Christopher Andersen
May	*Some Wildflower in My Heart*, Jamie Langston Turner
June	*Where the Heart Is*, Billie Letts [movie comparison night]
July	*The Covenant*, Beverly Lewis
August	*Blessings*, Anna Quindlen
September	*The Chocolate Side of Life*, Cindy Sigler Dagnan
October	*Future Homemakers of America*, Laurie Graham
November	*The Atonement Child*, Francine Rivers
December	Cookie exchange and book selection for next year
Sample Book Club List #3	
January	*To Kill a Mockingbird*, Harper Lee
February	*When Godly People Do Ungodly Things*, Beth Moore
March	*Flabbergasted*, Ray Blackston
April	*These High, Green Hills*, Jan Karon
May	*The Summons*, John Grisham
June	*The Book Club*, Mary Alice Monroe
July	*A Penny for Your Thoughts*, Mindy Starns Clark
August	*I Don't Know How She Does It*, Allison Pearson
September	*Let's Roll*, Lisa Beamer
October	*And the Shofar Blew*, Francine Rivers
November	*Sweet Caroline* (biography of Caroline Kennedy), Christopher Andersen
December	Book selection and book exchange party

Sample Book Club List #4	
January	*Catcher in the Rye*, J.D. Salinger
February	*The Power of a Praying Wife*, Stormie Omartian
March	*Out to Canaan*, Jan Karon
April	*Cinderella Rules*, Donna Kauffman
May	*Then Came Heaven*, LaVyrle Spencer
June	*The Secret Life of Bees*, Sue Monk Kidd
July	*After Anne*, Roxanne Henke
August	Double Feature for our trip: *Sister Chicks Do the Hula*, Robin Jones Gunn; *Delirious Summer*, Ray Blackston
September	*Diana's Boys, William and Harry and the Mother They Loved*, Christopher Andersen
October	*Boo*, Rene Gutteridge
November	*What a Girl Wants*, Kristin Billerbeck
December	Dinner/book exchange/book selection

As you can tell, we've grown inordinately fond of Christian fiction and the debate gets so heated, we've made this our largest reading category!

You Are Worth It

> "The ordinary acts we practice every day at home are of more importance to the soul than their simplicity might suggest."
>
> **Thomas Moore**

Although you may not be receiving a weekly or monthly paycheck anymore, you are still a working mother. It is doubly important to be rewarded for our sometimes unappreciated efforts. Below is a year's pay schedule of creative free or low-budget ways to stand in for a biweekly check. Have fun!

January, week 1. Wait until the children are down for the night or ask your husband to take over bedtime duties. For 20 minutes, soak in a luxurious bubble bath. Just for fun, add a bath fizzy or some Tub Tea. Bring every candle in the house into the bathroom with you and light them. No interruptions.

January, week 3. Browse one of the discount bookstores. To challenge yourself, set a budget of only $7. Purchase a current paperback bestseller, a few new magazines, find a hardback classic or other book. I've indulged in some buy-two-get-one-free sales on Nancy Drew's. After devouring the books in two nostalgic nights, I passed them along to my oldest daughter. Allow yourself 30 minutes of reading while curled up in your favorite chair with a steaming cup of hot cocoa.

February, week 1. Visit an old-fashioned candy store. Survey all the bins and treat yourself to an early valentine—a quarter pound of the most enticing thing you see, or your childhood favorite. You don't even have to share if you don't want to.

February, week 3. Go shopping with a friend for an especially pretty pair of panties. For fun, see what you can find for $5 or under. If you run into an incredible sale, you might even be able to swing a new nightie for under $15!

March, week 1. Cloister yourself in the bedroom or in your favorite room of the house. Walk down memory lane with the packet of ribbon-tied love letters from your courtship. Look through your hope chest or box of special keepsakes. Thumb through old yearbooks, scrapbooks and photo albums, thanking God for friends, memories, and irreplaceable treasures.

March, week 3. Indulge in a box of pretty spring stationery. Write a long, newsy letter to a friend you haven't been in touch with for a while. I know e-mail's quicker, but there is something joyous about getting a beautiful handwritten card or letter in the mailbox.

April, week 1. Rummage through the clearance table at the fabric store. Using fabric remnants, lace and ribbon, and a hot glue gun (the female version of duct tape), spruce up an old basket. Use it to hold makeup, stationery, or lotions.

April, week 3. When you're at the grocery store, buy one of the tiny pots of tulips or daffodils. Place it on a doily for an inexpensive centerpiece. Or place it near the kitchen window where it can brighten your day while you work.

May, week 1. Color an invitation and invite a friend over for a formal tea while your children nap or play together. Bring out your best teacups and saucers. Bake cookies, muffins, brownies, or lemon poppy seed bread. Drink up the leisure and companionship.

May, week 3. Be a child again. Go outside and blow bubbles. Get the pail of sidewalk chalk and draw pictures or leave a message on the sidewalk for school-age children to see when they arrive home.

June, week 1. As days become hot, try this treat: Wet your finger with water and run it over the rim of a crystal or glass goblet. Dip the rim in sugar. Chill the glass in the freezer. After 20-30 minutes fill the glass with pink lemonade. Sit outside on the porch or patio and enjoy!

June, week 3. Place glow-in-the-dark stars in constellations or random patterns on your bedroom ceiling. After dark, have a romantic picnic/ stargazing session with your husband.

July, week 1. Buy a fabric-bound blank book in festive stars-n-stripes or a pretty summer floral. Begin to jot down what you love about your life;

complain only slightly about what you don't love. Include special family memories and the adorable things your kids say and do.

July, week 3. During naptime, bake a batch of brownies. Sneak a spoonful (or two) of batter and then lick the bowl.

August, week 1. It's time for back to school and new beginnings. Buy or rent an exercise tape that you truly enjoy and begin doing the workout three times per week. It boosts energy, self-esteem, overall health, and you'll enjoy better-fitting clothes. Toddlers will love pretending to go through the motions with you. Soup cans or water bottles work great for toddler "weights."

August, week 3. Bring out that stationery that you purchased in March. For each of your children, write a letter, explaining to them what you love about them. Include a few special memories unique to that child. Give it to them when they come home from school or save it to give to them on a future special day. While you're at it, write a love letter to your husband and place it on his pillow. You'll glow in the warmth of appreciation for all your blessings.

September, week 1. At this week's trip to the grocery store, linger over the magazine section. Choose one that's filled with fall decorating, recipe, or craft ideas (whichever one appeals to you). Take it home and browse through it during any spare minutes. Clip and save ideas you like, and start a dream file. Try a new recipe this week.

September, week 3. As you settle into the routine of school, errands, and chores, stop at the park and play for 15 minutes. Swing on the swings. Slide down the slide. If you're brave, see if you can still cross the monkey bars. Play. If the kids are with you, you'll reap the benefits of surprising them with an unexpected treat while reawakening your childlike side.

October, week 1. On a sunny, Indian summer day, bundle toddlers and infants into strollers and take a brisk walk. Collect colored leaves and place some in a crystal bowl for this week's centerpiece. Save a few to press in the pages of your journal (from July). Help older children make leaf rubbings with crayons, wax paper, and the iron.

October, week 3. Trade a college student a home-cooked meal and several loads of clean laundry for a few hours of free babysitting. Use this time to window shop, meet a friend for lunch, or spend time haunting your favorite antique, craft, or hobby shop.

November, week 1. In your journal this week write down five things every night you're thankful for. Begin looking in your files or at the library for a simple new craft idea. When you've got it, make two of them—one to enjoy and one to share with your mother, a friend, or neighbor.

November, week 3. On one of your trips to the grocery store, buy an inexpensive bouquet of fresh cut flowers or a pot of autumn mums. Arrange the flowers in a pretty vase or snip off the stems and float them in a bowl. Put them on your kitchen or coffee table or a bedroom dresser as a reminder of life outdoors.

December, week 1. Take a snow day. Curl up by the biggest window of your home with a cup of cocoa, hot tea, or flavored coffee. Simply be still. Reflect. Later, if it's deep enough, dress warmly, catch snowflakes on your tongue, and make a few snow angels.

December, week 3. While you're out in the holiday bustle, sign up for one of those cosmetic counter makeovers. Most larger department stores offer them for free or for a minimal purchase. Go shopping for a special tree ornament just for you. Choose a style that delights you. Victorian. Country. Glitzy. Handmade. Rejoice in the blessing of the season and being home as you place it on the tree.

Having these little perks to look forward to each month can be a sanity-saver and an affirmation of the incredible importance of what you're doing—shaping and molding the future. I talked to one mom who makes an annual pilgrimage to one of her town's nicer hotels. She gets a room for one night and packs her favorite jammies, a great book, her Bible, a notebook, and a few great movies and hunkers down for the night. She uses the time to recharge her spiritual life and her batteries, making lists of goals and plans for the coming year. The uninterrupted night's sleep and the feeling of playing hooky refreshes her and complements her skills as wife and mother during the hectic days. I like that idea so much, I'm thinking about doing the same thing at a not-too-distant bed-and-breakfast next autumn.

As you get the hang of mommy time and enjoying a little reward without feeling guilty, add to this list with your own wonderful creativity.

The biggest thrills will be those spontaneous hugs from your toddler; the afternoon spent laughing and making a mess in the kitchen while baking cookies with your children; that warm and cozy morning smile from your infant; the tender look in your husband's eyes that tells you more than words ever could.

In my mind's eye I can look ahead into the hazy, but not-so-distant future. Children grown. Returning from college with luggage, boyfriends, empty wallets, and happy hearts. But only for a visit. We'll giggle and reminisce, but it will never be the same. So in between catching that mommy time, cherish each moment you have today. I know I will.

> "We pray, O God, that You will slow us down, for we know that we live too fast...Make us take time to live."
>
> **Peter Marshall**

QUESTIONS FOR STUDY AND REFLECTION

1. Write down the top three objections that come to mind whenever

you contemplate having mommy time. Make two more columns. In the second column, next to each objection, write down how that objection could be overcome by the benefits of taking mommy time. In the third column, jot down an idea for letting go of that objection.

2. Look at Matthew 8:23; 12:1; 14:22-25; 15:21; and 26:36. In each case, Jesus withdrew either alone or with friends, for different reasons. Summarize in one or two sentences how Jesus felt about the value of retreat.

3. Read 1 Corinthians 3:16. How can that principle apply to taking mommy time?

4. Some of what prevents our mommy moments from being relaxing and productive is the constant state of planning, plotting, and worry. Take a few moments and read Matthew 6:25-34. Read it again in *The Message*. Write down your top five worries on scraps of paper. Now give each one to God in prayer and then rip them up or burn them as a physical reminder that they have been turned over to the only One who can do anything about them.

5. If time and money were no object, what retreat, spa day, or trip would you take as mommy time?

6. Read Matthew 10:29-31. List at least two specific ways that God has remembered you or provided for you during the last year.

Action Plan

Start saving now. For a small treat, get a manicure—many places give them for $10-$15, and a good one can last up to 10 days—or save for a new hairstyle or hair accessory. Or save for a more long-term, bigger treat like a 30-minute massage ($30 to

$60), spa treatment ($35 to $60), or full spa day ($100 to $300). Look for seasonal specials that combine a manicure, haircut and style, and massage for as little as $75. Drop hints that gift certificates for such items would be most welcome! During a really tight budget month, invite a group of girlfriends over to give each other deep condition treatments, manicures, pedicures, or facials.

Meanwhile, start carving out ten minutes a day that are all yours. Read one chapter from a great book. Take in three magazine articles. Disappear into a deep bubble bath and relax to music or take the book in with you.

Journal

Write one paragraph about the perfect mommy day. Take your mind back to elementary school when the teacher would assign short essay topics and let your imagination run wild!

Memorize

"I have loved you with an everlasting love; I have drawn you with loving-kindness" (Jeremiah 31:3).

Chapter 9

Making Peace with Your AC (After-Children) Life and Body

A mommy's critical fashion concerns: "It has to be comfortable, even during my PMS week; it has to be machine washable; it has to be free of any beads, flowers, or sharp buttons that would impale any child who needs a hug or to be carried to bed; it can't wrinkle so badly during carpool that I look like I've slept in my car; it has to be easily removed so that I can go potty several hundred times a day; it can't give me a wedgie, can't show my midriff, and it has to make me look thinner than I really am."

—Vicki Iovine, author of The Girlfriends' Guide
to Surviving the First Year of Motherhood

Trapped. Stuck. Caged. Bland. Frumpy. Dull. Edgy. Derailed. Cranky. Hardly good copy for an enticing personal ad. But it's how a lot of moms that I meet while speaking at conferences describe how they feel about themselves and life at times. None of them regret their decisions, they just want to know how to stay current, maintain good relationships, preserve their sanity and, perhaps, someday return to their formal education or careers. Oh, and how to bring about some peace with the changes they saw in the mirror. Motherhood and father time can both wreak havoc on our BC (before-children) bodies—and this without the current parade of extreme makeovers and constant focus the media places on physical appearance.

The Issue of Self-Esteem

One of the biggest challenges for stay-at-home moms is the loss of self-esteem. In his book *Women Leaving the Workplace*, Larry Burkett labels this as "self disapproval." We, who once held positions in the workforce or at least contributed in a tangible way to the family coffers, now struggle with our sense of worth. After so many conversations with preschoolers, days spent with Barney, Pooh, and yes, even Veggie Tales, one longs for an extended period of adult conversation, while simultaneously dreading an evening out for fear of bursting out with an Eeyoresque, "Oh, dear, my tail seems to have fallen off again." Or at least a pitiful chorus of "Oh, Where Is My Hairbrush?" It's one of the reasons that some of the mommy-daddy Visa commercials are uproariously entertaining; if anyone would stop a limousine (assuming we had one for the evening) at an all-night convenience store for a diaper run, it would be one of us!

We struggle with our esteem because society tells us that it is derived from what we *do*. As one mother of three put it, "Society puts a lot of pressure on us to hold a paying job to really be worth anything." Sadly, that's all too true. My wonderful friend and college roommate, Debbie, who is also the mother of three wrote: "The worst thing is feeling taken for granted. People say things that hurt like, 'Oh, you're just at home.' Or, 'Since you're not working could you do…?' This creates a lack of self-esteem and confidence."

I know what she means. When I worked full-time outside the home, I received pity, knowing looks, and sometimes, outright condemnation from mothers who were at home. But I also received tangible items of esteem: a monthly paycheck from whence came actual money; praise from my boss; comradeship from colleagues; interaction with lively students. I anticipated a perfect balance when I quit to stay home. After all, I had recently been in the professional world, surely I could ride the fence and please both sides. Ha! It is sometimes difficult to explain my decision to others when I see the response to the social question: "What do *you* do?" The glazed look or curt dismissals when you proudly say, "I stay at home with my children," are hurtful.

Of course, the real answer to that question—"I do fifty loads of laundry, feed and walk the dog, change thirty-seven diapers, load the dishwasher, fix lunch, unload the dishwasher, begin dinner, fill the dishwasher again, volunteer too much, pay the bills, build block towers, balance a one-woman answering service, scrub toilets, fold clothes, read stories, rock babies, change sheets, grocery shop, take forgotten lunches and library books to school, sweep, mop, vacuum, and feel behind the entire time"—just doesn't seem all that glamorous. Neither does it begin to touch what I really do all day. I shape lives. I teach. I soothe. I listen. I cuddle. I play. I model. I laugh. I instill. All because I am *there*.

This lack in self-esteem became even more apparent to me while I was working on my first book for mothers. I talked to everyone from total strangers in the Wal-Mart parking lot to moms in the pediatric waiting room to other volunteer mothers at my kids' school. Their reaction to my immediate curiosity and genuine interest in them was pure surprise—"You want to talk to *me?*" I asked questions—and boy, did they talk! One mother returned my survey and expanded it to three pages, typewritten! Still, everyone affirmed that the benefits of staying home far outweighed the sacrifices.

I talked to mothers who had been lawyers, computer programmers, executive secretaries, marketing managers, accountants, school teachers, college professors, nurses, doctors' assistants, dental hygienists, and store managers. At one point most of the women sitting in the gymnastics waiting room were filling out surveys! Most of these women had college degrees; none of them felt they were wasting their education. The common refrain was, "I can always go back, but my kids won't always be little." Your children will only be *this* age once. Time doesn't stop, and you can't run fast enough to catch it and bring it back. So the bottom line is, we *know* we're doing a good thing by being mommies; we're just not sure how to reconcile it with the fact that we're also women, wives, lovers, and intelligent human beings.

And by the Way—What Happened to My Body?

Perhaps it's time for a reality check. In my book *The Chocolate Side of Life*, I did the math, "The average woman is 5'4", 140 pounds, and wears a size 12-14. Yet the typical model is 5'9" and 110 pounds. That translates to a size 2-4!" Most of us can spout similar statistics. We know the facts with our heads; we just can't accept them with our hearts.

I won't bother telling you that self-image or even the image you project to others isn't important. I wouldn't fool you; I wouldn't even be fooling myself! I do believe that we need to put it into perspective and fast. What would life be like for you if you weren't always trying to make the mirror happy? If you truly believed that beauty started from within and radiated outward? 'Cause guess what? It does!

In a survey conducted by *Family Circle* magazine, Senior Editor Ginni Wallace attempted to concretely measure the overall happiness factor and mental health of families. There were a few common denominators among those who rated themselves as the happiest. They included having strong faith, optimistic spirits, knowing their closest neighbors, feeling connected in their communities, belonging to a church or mosque or synagogue, being registered voters and actually voting, being happy with their number of friends, practicing mutual respect within the family, and having at least a small savings. In short, their happiness factor reflected their level of *contentment*. Corrie Ten Boom, an author and concentration camp survivor, used to say that worry is "carrying tomorrow's burden with today's strength." Isn't that what we're doing when we're worrying about how we measure up? We are forever caught in the comparison trap.

No Comparison

The longer I'm at this motherhood thing, the more I realize that you can't compare, not even your present self to your former self. This month my oldest daughter, now officially a teenager, was asked to complete a scrapbook "Story of Me," which covered her entire life thus far. We scrounged for pictures and she wrote copy for each year. What astounded me almost as much as the changes from her infancy to adolescence were the changes in myself, particularly my body. I found myself muttering under my breath. *I can't believe that was me! Look how thin and tan I was! I was actually in shape. Even after the first two children, I bounced back fairly quickly.* But gradually, the pictures were pointing out the march of time. An indefinable oldness crept around the edges of my eyes, a softness around my belly. Chagrined, I watched the Trace Adkins music video "One Hot Mama" with some friends and reminded myself of two important things. First, I would not trade what I have now even if I could redeem that earlier figure, and second, the silly song is probably a more accurate picture of what our spouses truly believe. As long as we're trying, as long as we're available to them, their eyes look at us with flattering, soft-focus lenses. In short, making peace with our AC bodies involves *accepting* them ourselves.

For all of the flaws I could readily point out on my body, I don't have stretch marks. I remarked to a close friend in the church restroom one day about that and being the gregarious sort, she hiked up her shirt a few inches and pointed to red and silvery dashes swirled all over her belly. "I hate you," she joked. But then she related how one night her husband had placed his hand over her stretch marks and said, "Don't worry about these. I love them, because you got them carrying our son." All together now: "Awwwww!" See what I mean? Husbands really are on our side!

If you find yourself at a higher level of contentment until you compare your body to a supermodel (or to your best friend who just lost 15 pounds) or until you look around your toy-strewn family room and walk around its edges, skirting the massive amounts of toy army men, headless Barbies, and building blocks decorating the floor, and compare it to the beautiful layout in *Country Living*, then you're trapped. If your child isn't yet an independent reader and the other mothers on your committee proudly report that their youngsters are reading above grade level and you're secretly ashamed or, worse still, you scold your child rather than encourage him, you're trapped. If you feel frumpy every time you see certain members of the "muffia" (Supermoms, at least in appearance, who never go anywhere without professionally done nails, matching handbags, sporting the latest haircut, and spouting their child's endless list of activities, making you feel like a slug in comparison), it's nearly hopeless. Except for one big factor—God. You see, we were made in His image, remember? How bad could it be?

Feeling Content

If it helps, studies have shown that most people have a happiness set point, similar to our natural weight. Achieving a material goal, like a vacation, raise, promotion, or new furniture, boosts happiness temporarily, for about six months. Even getting whatever it is we think we want won't solve the problem. It has to come from the Source of contentment.

In 1900 the average lifespan was 47 years old. Today, the nation's fastest growing age group is the centenarians. Yep, those who've lived to the ripe old age of 100 years. The landmark study, *Living to 100: Lessons in Living to Your Maximum Potential at Any Age* by Thomas T. Peris, M.D. and Margery Hutter Silver, Ed.D., demonstrates that while luck and genetics do play a part, the inner spirit, including healthy doses of humor and the determination of a person, plays an even larger role. Nearly all the centenarians ate healthfully and remained active, both physically and mentally. Helen Boardman, in her memoirs entitled *105 and Counting*, said, "I think the mind has a lot to do with the way you feel." I know she's right.

Fred Hale—112 years old in 2003—teases his physical therapist each time he says, "See you tomorrow." "Perhaps," comes the reply, "I'm not making any long-term plans." That cracks me up. It's all about perspective. I have one lone year left before the dreaded mammogram era—I am officially 39. I'm not necessarily looking forward to it, nor have I embraced all the changes my body is determined to make, but it's a lot better than the alternative!

Improving Our Outlook on Life and Self

Now that you've gotten the philosophy and the pep talk, let's look at some quick practical ways you can improve your smile, your funny bone, your body, your mind, and your attitude.

We'll look a bit more into beauty and fitness later as it relates to the grow, glow, guard principles in your marriage. In this chapter, though, I want to focus on habits you can adopt that can change your outlook and your countenance while providing tangible pick-me-ups every day.

Physical Beautifiers

- *Drink that water.* I'll mention this again and again. First thing in the morning, put eight rubber bands around your wrist, one for each eight-ounce glass of water you should be drinking each day. As you gulp one down, remove one band.

- *Green tea is a great way to begin or end your day.* (Lipton makes some palatable blends, if you're not a big fan). The medical community is touting its health benefits.

- *Fruit juice is another good choice,* but it's even better to eat fresh fruit. Try putting a splash of juice in your water or diluting your juice one-third to one-half with water to cut down on liquid calories.

+ *Eating a fresh grapefruit half can boost your metabolism* slightly and aid in needed weight loss.

+ *Don't skimp on the calcium.* Not only do we women need that for healthy teeth and bones, but calcium has been proven to aid in weight loss. Just stick with skim, or 1 percent milk, or low fat string cheese for snacks.

+ *Even five dropped pounds, if you're overweight, can make a big difference* in your energy levels and how hard your heart has to work. It eases stress on joints and improves sleep quality. No diet tricks can beat the old-fashioned discipline of portion control and exercise, though. Sorry.

+ *Take off your makeup and wash your face every night.* No exceptions. Follow with a mild toner or astringent. Exfoliate gently every few days, more frequently if you have oily skin. Follow with a nighttime moisturizer.

+ *Incorporate some simple routines to help take care of you.* For example, use a pore strip on your nose on Tuesday nights and a facial mask on Friday nights. Once a week, use a deep conditioner on your hair. During the summer, rinse your hair weekly with cold water or cider vinegar for shine, following your normal wash.

+ *I know, I know—who thinks about their monthly breast exam?* But not only should you, one director of the American Cancer Society (Debbie Salslow, director of breast and gynecologic cancers) says that there might be an easier method. Instead of the circular pattern, try using a technique called the vertical strips method. Imagine that your breast is a grid. Use the pads of your three middle fingers and work in tiny circles up and down each grid from the collarbone to under each breast. Do your exam at the same time each month and do a visual check in the mirror from the front and sides too, with arms up over your head and then down at your sides.

+ *Schedule your yearly exam for your birthday month.* While you're at it, make a dermatology appointment for a full body skin cancer screening.

+ *Whenever your skin is extra dry, apply baby oil* to shower-damp skin and then slather on your regular lotion. Treat yourself to special seasonal scented lotions too. Try vanilla or caramel for winter, apple for autumn, citrus for spring, and coconut for summer. For an extra special treat try Burt's Baby Bee Apricot Oil.

+ *Sleep, sleep, sleep.* Use the nap plan. Turn in early a few nights a week. Not only does sleep keep your hormone levels more even, thus controlling mood swings, it's good for your complexion (skin and body functions rejuvenate during sleep). Besides, sleep deprivation can make you fat! It induces production of the stress hormone, cortisol, which contributes to stored fat. Also, chronic sleep-deprivation causes a lengthening of reaction time, similar to that of drivers who drink. It is too dangerous to be driving around tired with our precious cargo.

Stress

Stress may be literally killing Americans, and it can hit wives and mothers especially hard. Shelley Taylor, Ph.D., author of *The Tending Instinct,* writes that while husbands may be fed, clothed, and picked up after, the caretaker (usually the wife) may suffer. "When men arrive home from work, their stress hormone levels gradually decline....In contrast, women's stress hormones often remain on high alert long into the evening."[1] Aside from the nurturing nature of women, living in America may also add to this. The average American uses 10.2 days of vacation time a year; in western Europe, four weeks are mandated by law! The afternoon siesta and extended, relaxed family dinners are still in full force in Italy also. For us mothers, work tends to last all day, every day. I say, stay here enjoying the benefits of our wonderful nation and when it comes to time off, pretend you're in Europe!

The negative effects of stress are well-documented. It speeds up heart rate and respiration and raises blood pressure and body temperature. It can affect our appetite, metabolism, and sex drive. It can halt menstruation, bring on panic attacks, and some newer studies even show that high stress levels during pregnancy can make a woman's children more sensitive to stress. And we've all experienced the uncanny way in which infants latch onto our moods and mirror them. Of course, good stress can instigate the fight or flight response, saving us from danger, or stimulate adrenaline to get us through the last of a difficult phase or project, but long term, it's deadly.

For women, disturbing side effects include broken sleep—trouble falling asleep and staying asleep, and brooding. Okay, worrying. Susan Nolen-Hoeksema, Ph.D., found that this pattern of overthinking is primarily relegated to the young and middle-aged. In fact adults over 65 "had a lot of trouble understanding what I was describing."[2] No matter that they had been through wars, depressions, demanding jobs, and loss of their life's mates, when asked if they found themselves dwelling on those experiences and feeling sad or anxious, they seemed surprised. "Not often," and "That wouldn't be a helpful thing to do, would it?" were typical responses. Perhaps we need to latch ourselves to an older woman mentor and beg her to let us in on her wisdom and experience. For how we cope with stress can determine the length of our lives and how well we live them.

Stress Reducers

+ *Sleep.* Here we go again, right? Not really, it's in the top five ways to beat stress. How can you get to sleep when millions of thoughts and runaway to-do lists haunt your evenings?

+ *Don't exercise or drink caffeine* closer than three hours before bedtime.

+ *Do have sex,* however. The intimacy and natural crash can induce an awesome sleep.

+ *Light a vanilla- or lavender-scented candle* half an hour before bedtime; studies show that both scents induce relaxation.

+ *Read your Bible*, unwind with a book and/or those devotions with your husband, rather than watch TV, which stimulates rather than relaxes.

+ *Go to bed as close to the same time as possible each night.* Don't let your bedtime or wake-up time vary by more than an hour to an hour and a half on weekends; it will make weekdays that much harder.

+ *Make your bedroom a haven*, an oasis, a respite. Keep it clutter-free. Use the planning principles we cover in this book to make your room a place to unwind and to love.

+ *Don't discuss stressful topics just before bed* (finances, worries, and so on); not only should you not talk about these in your bedroom, but problems seem to be magnified at night.

+ *Pray*, making sure to ask God to guard even your dreams.

+ *Keep a small pad of paper and pen on your nightstand* so that if you're worried about forgetting something, you can write it down and release that thought from waking you up. Try the same thing with all of your worries. Write worries down, pray about them, then tear them up and trust God to handle them. Try making a list of the next day's tasks several hours before retiring so your mind will let go.

+ *Sleep in a room with as cool a temperature as your budget and family ages allow.* While an infant can't be in a nursery that's too cold, remember that unduly warm temperatures, clothing, or bulky blankets have been linked to SIDS. For the rest of us, many studies show that cold sleeping temperatures with the blankets piled on are the best for a great night's sleep.

+ *Exercise.* It's great for reducing stress, easing monthly cramps, and boosting endorphins, which help your mood. If you have stairs, take them two at a time to tone the thighs and firm the rear. Do wall sits while talking on the phone. Do five minutes worth of gentle stretching and ten minutes worth of free-weight lifting in the mornings to jumpstart your metabolism (bicep curls, hammers, side arm raises). Do leg lifts or crunches during a favorite show.

+ *Walking can give the same benefit as jogging,* without the damage to your knees. Get your heart rate up, move quickly. Use the time to think, daydream, clear your head, pray. To motivate yourself, try listening to a book on tape so you'll be dying to know the rest of the story. Check out Jan Karon's *At Home in Mitford.* Walk with a buddy for accountability.

+ *Go ahead and fidget.* Studies show that toe tappers, finger drummers, knee swingers, and hair twirlers weigh less than their non-fidgeting counterparts.

+ *Make doing something pleasurable for yourself a priority each day.* You'll be a better wife and mother for it. Taking care of yourself and your health is a great place to start.

+ *Great posture and tonal dressing can pare pounds visually.* But don't just go with basic black, consider chocolate and navy too. Add a shot of color: fuchsia with black, bright orange with chocolate, and lime green with navy.

+ *Apply your makeup with upward and outward strokes, never downward.* Don't prop your face in your hands, either. These actions pull and bunch skin and induce wrinkles.

+ *Wear SPF-15 minimum sunscreen* on your face, hands, and neck year-round.

+ *Get friends of a variety of ages and interests.* Sign up with a mentor. Those who have a wide circle of friends statistically get sick from annoyances like the common cold much less frequently than those who are loners.

+ *Pursue a hobby*, take a class, and cultivate an interest new to you. A fulfilled and motivated woman is intriguing and has more energy.

+ *Don't neglect inner beauty.* Your spiritual component and your servant side need nurturing. "Try going through an entire day asking yourself what you'd do if your goal were to be helpful rather than efficient," wrote author Mira Kirshenbaum in her book *The Emotional Energy Factor.* Did you catch that, precious, efficient type A's? I write that with much love for you.

+ *Laugh.* Laughter is a superb ab-toner, stress reducer, and inner beautifier. Share the fun by playing with your kids, watching old home movies together, or indulging in your own silly rituals.

Body Image, Lifestyle Changes, and Intimacy

When a woman feels desirable physically, she is liable to be an outstanding, giving, and more adventurous lover. Work toward it, but also pray about it. No, it's not a misprint—ask God to give you a proper respect for yourself and your body. Acknowledge that being both a parent and a wife is draining. Choose to focus on your marriage and help bless it by being the confident, beautiful woman God intended.

+ *Get your husband to pitch in.* A more relaxed wife is a more receptive one, plus it has hidden benefits. Scott Coltrane, Ph.D., a professor of sociology at the University of California, Riverside, analyzed data from more than 3,000 families. One thing they found is that kids whose dads help perform household chores are more likely to get along with peers and less likely to be school troublemakers. "Seeing men perform domestic duties teaches children cooperation and democratic family values," says Coltrane.[3]

+ *Occasionally be both the initiator and the aggressor in sex.* It can be a surprising turn-on to feel in control. Read up on the subject and try new tricks. Many husbands like the rear-entry position for variety. Experts recommend you stack one or two pillows under your stomach as you lie on the bed, to ease back strain and allow easier entry.

+ *Head to the candle shop, dry some flowers, or bake a pie!* In research conducted by the Smell-Taste Treatment and Research Foundation, the scents of pumpkin pie and lavender increased male arousal more than any of the other 30 scents tested.[4]

+ *Give a gift.* In England there's a tradition called Tuesday gift. Gifts are exchanged for no reason. Surprise your man with tickets to a movie, concert, or sporting event he's been wanting to attend. Or better yet, invite him to your bedroom on Tuesday night for playtime with the new, improved you!

+ *Kiss, kiss, kiss.* Not only does that rev up passion, but one German study found that giving or receiving a goodbye kiss on the way out the door every morning is associated with prolonged life, a reduced number of missed work days, and even fewer auto accidents on the way to work![5] So much from such a simple gesture.

+ *Mark the trail.* If your husband is coming home late and the kids are safely tucked in, start shedding your clothing in the kitchen or by the back door and leave a welcome trail all the way up to your bedroom. Wait for him there in a room blazing with candles—and desire!

+ *Keep the grapes in good shape.* Song of Solomon speaks of "little foxes that spoil the vineyards." Check for whining, discontent, perfectionism, taking things for granted, selfishness, nagging, impatience—if you find them in your vineyard, set about evicting them in short order.

You've Got to Have a Dream

Take a few moments to write down goals for yourself in several areas: personal, marriage, family, spiritual, career, financial, dream. Under each goal write down at least three practical steps that will help you realize the goal. For example: Under personal, if your goals are to get in better shape and lose five pounds, don't let them remain that vague. Write: exercise 15 minutes a day this week, cut down refined sugar to twice a week. Then increase the intensity of each step. Exercise 20 minutes, then 30; eventually limit refined sugar to one day a week, during holidays, and vacations.

And *do* dream. While you're at it, dream *big*. Dream God-sized dreams. Think about what you would do if time and money were no object. Work toward those dreams, and as you do, don't forget to be faithful in the small things.

Keep Your Friendships

While God needs to be our best friend, and our husband, our best *earthly* friend, we still need to nurture and cultivate girlfriends. It is unfair and unrealistic to expect our husbands to meet all of our needs, particularly that of excruciatingly detailed conversation; most men still want "just the facts, ma'am." We need girfriends. One of mine recently sent me this e-mail which summed up the intricate intertwining of female lives.

> *Girlfriends bring casseroles and*
> *scrub your bathroom when you are sick.*
> *Girlfriends keep your children and your secrets.*
> *Girlfriends give advice when you ask for it.*
> *Sometimes you take it, sometimes you don't.*
> *Girlfriends don't always tell you that you're right,*
> *but they're usually honest.*
> *Girlfriends still love you, even when they*
> *don't agree with your choices.*

Girlfriends might send you a birthday card,
but they might not. It does not matter in the least.

Girlfriends laugh with you and
you don't need canned jokes to start the laughter.
Girlfriends pull you out of jams.
Girlfriends don't keep a calendar that
lets them know who hosted the other last.
Girlfriends will give a party for your son or daughter
when they get married or have a baby.

Moreover, girlfriends are there for you, in an instant and truly,
when the hard times come.
Girlfriends listen when you lose a job or a husband.
Girlfriends listen when your mind and body fail.
My girlfriends bless my life. Once we were young, with no idea
of the incredible joys or the incredible sorrows that lay ahead.
Nor did we know how much we would need each other.

—Unknown

Please don't think I have it all together. Don't think that I'm never mopey on days when I unzip my jeans and find that my stomach has been pleated with semi-permanent accordion shapes, that I can't still be undone by something as shallow as a bad hair day, that I waltz around our home whistling Broadway tunes and slow dancing with my husband the second he walks in the door. Do I some days? Sure. But can I increase those good days by a long margin? You bet. Why? My faith and hope in God. Hope gives us wings to fly through days that are grounded in reality. I've put in my request with Greg that I absolutely must be buried with good hair, and my gracious heavenly Father has promised us all perfect bodies in heaven.

Next summer I will turn 40. I still can't believe I am putting this on paper that will be in print. Nevertheless, I will be traveling, along with six wonderful friends, to a beach on a Texas coast. We're going to celebrate my birthday, have book club on the beach, bare our souls, and yes, allow each other the dubious privilege of being seen in our (gulp!) bathing suits. We plan to eat lots of chocolate, saunter on sandy beaches, kick in the water (with no one demanding leg lifts), wear plenty of red and lime green, discuss life, and oh, yes, *live* it.

Questions for Study and Reflection

1. Read 1 Peter 3:3-4 and 1 Samuel 16:7. Although we know this to be true, why is it that we remain focused on outward appearance, both our own and those of others?

2. Read Isaiah 53:2 which speaks of Jesus. Why did God choose to send Him to earth without that particular type of "glory"? What is the lesson there for us?

3. Read Proverbs 31:10-31. How many verses make reference to her physical appearance? How many verses refer to her work ethic? Her character? Her personality? Her relationships (especially to husband and children)? Make columns for each category and list them.

4. Fill in the blanks for Proverbs 31:30. "_____ is ____ _____, and beauty is _____; but a woman who _____ the _____ is to be _____." Are you someone who could be praised for that?

5. Have you noticed a difference in your actions or attitude on days when you feel less than pretty? Are they cyclical or situational?

6. Reread study question 2. Have you ever known someone whom you believed to be beautiful until you were around them more?

Conversely, do you know someone who would not be considered conventionally beautiful but whom you regard as pretty because of their actions? What do you think others say about you?

Action Plan

Choose one healthy thing to do for yourself every week this month, one day at a time. For example, choose to drink the eight glasses of water every day for one week. Don't think beyond that first day and don't add anything to it until the next week. Move more than you have been moving. Don't think dieting, think changing...by small steps...the habits that can give you renewed esteem, energy, and outlook.

Journal

Keep track of your moods and what you think caused them. Also keep track of the healthy changes you are incorporating into your lifestyle and how well you think they're working. In the back of your journal, consider recording your beginning measurements and then again after 21 days of your new exercise and lifestyle changes. The progress can inspire you to continue on toward your goal.

Memorize

"You created my inmost being; you knit me together in my mother's womb. I praise you because I am fearfully and wonderfully made; your works are wonderful, I know that full well" (Psalm 139:13-14).

Chapter 10

The Spiritual Dimension

When you teach your son,
you teach your son's son.

—*The Talmud*

"These commandments that I give
you today are to be upon your hearts.
Impress them on your children. Talk about
them when you sit at home and when you
walk along the road, when you lie down
and when you get up....Write them on the
doorframes of your houses
and on your gates."

—*Deuteronomy 6:6-7,9*

It's a heart-stoppingly terrifying, wonderful, awe-full thought: God has entrusted us with the responsibility of teaching our children about Him! Using the verse above, I believe God has given us the very best formula for doing just that. It begins by being so close to God that talking to Him is as natural as breathing air; that including Him in your life is as delightful as being in the company of a dear friend. "These commandments that I give you today are to be upon your hearts." If they aren't on our hearts, we can't very well share them with our children.

While browsing through one of our local Bible bookstores, I recently picked up a 99-cent 5 x 7 postcard. It's a print from artist Nathan Green entitled simply *Family Worship*. It depicts a family, complete with a golden retriever like ours, gathered around the fireplace for devotions. The dad is reading from God's Word in a rocking chair, a little one with footie pajamas, clutching a teddy bear, sits on his lap. The mom is leaning in to listen. One child is listening intently, face tilted upward in the twilight, a boyish arm thrown around his dog. Yet another child in a precious pair of drop-seat jammies is curled up on the floor with a beloved blanket. Jesus is seated on the floor next him, gazing at him with infinite tenderness. His pierced hand rests on the little boy's shoulder. It drew me in the moment I spotted it and a few days later I snatched up a simple, sturdy frame for it at Target. God went with me, I'm sure.

I wanted it for three reasons. First, I probably can't afford the huge version of the print, and I have always used postcards and calendar pictures as art. It's amazing how wonderful they look in a frame. Second, I wanted a constant visual, movable reminder that Jesus is truly with me in all I do. Third, I want to introduce it during our family nights this year (I'll probably use it every week, just like I do my daddy's old popcorn bowl) so that my girls will realize, perhaps in a more tangible way, that Jesus laughs, loves them, and is so willing to participate in the wonderful chaos of our family life if only we'll invite Him! To truly grasp that concept gives me goose pimples!

If you've ever spoken to yourself out loud (and where are the mothers who haven't), then it's just a hop, skip, and jump from there to dialoging all day long with God. "Pray without ceasing," (1 Thessalonians 5:17 NKJV) Scripture admonishes us. It seems daunting; darn near impossible. But all it really means is to be in conversation with God. That's right, conversation. I know it seems presumptuous to tell the God of the universe about our need for new brakes on the car, the tiff with our husband, and our bone-tired weariness, but He wants to hear. He desires to help. He deserves our thanks, our praise, our trust. In chapter 3 we talked about connecting with God first thing in the morning. In this chapter, I want to go a bit deeper, laying the groundwork for time with God and modeling a spiritual example for our kids. Spirituality isn't for Sundays only. It isn't churchy, nor is it preachy. It is the simple recognition that because we were created as spiritual beings, Christianity affects and permeates everything that we do. Some of the simplest acts you'll perform all day are spiritual expressions. It's not a matter of putting on spiritual armor; it's a matter of never taking it off!

Make every effort to get involved in a MOPS (Mothers of Preschoolers) group, a Moms In Touch prayer group, or a Bible Study Fellowship group. Most of these groups have separate special activities for your children. You gain adult fellowship, accountability, and time in God's Word. At the very least, get together with another mom, choose a book to study, and covenant to meet once each week to go through the book, read the accompanying Scriptures, and pray for and with each other.

Pray, pray, pray. Trace each of your children's hands on sturdy paper. Write the things you want to pray over them in the center of each hand. When they're absent from you at school, place your hand on top of their handprint and pray. If you have a husband who is often absent for business, do the same with his hand. Occasionally slip into their room at night and pray over them after they're asleep. Get on your knees often and literally. Of course, tucking them in and hearing their prayers is a blessing.

Ways to Pray

I am terrible at praying while sitting still or lying down. If I sit, my mind wanders. I hear the dryer buzzer go off and my prayer goes something like this: *God, please be with the missionaries in Taiwan. Guide them and give them opportunities...to make their clothes soft and static free! I really ought to go fold those now before wrinkles set in...I'm sorry God, now where was I?* Ugh. What a pathetic way to address my Creator. If I'm lying down and trying to pray, like any mother who is still for more than 49 seconds, I'm asleep.

So last year I began my favorite way to pray. I purchased a multi-colored package of index cards. I chose one color for daily prayers and other colors for each day of the week. My daily cards have some constants and some variations. For example, I pray for my husband, my children, the soldiers in Iraq, myself, and Baby Silas, a precious neighbor's baby, for whom I committed myself to daily prayer when he was born with a severe kidney malfunction. I scribble additional items and cross them off as they're answered. Sometimes I need to add another request just for a week, or for a specific time period when that need will be met.

I won't give you the entire litany of all of my requests, but I will say it's easier to link them to certain days, if possible. For example, I pray for our ministers, their work, their marriages, and their walk with God on Sundays; on Mondays, I do the same for my book club gals, since that's the day of the week that we meet; on Thursdays I pray for my women's Bible study group, since that's our day; Saturdays I reserve for various ministries, missionaries, and church family needs; on Friday one of my cards simply reads, *Extra praise!* That's always fun. I prayed for the 2004 elections most fervently, and after thanking God for the outcome, I now pray for the leaders that are in office. Pray for your extended family, for nations, for God's will, for your neighbors.

I have rubber banded these cards together, and every day, March through October, I walk two miles and pray out loud. As I walk by certain homes, I pray for those that we know: the girls' playmates, a few of their teachers. Elexa goes along in her stroller, holds the cards for me when I'm finished, and then conducts her own sort of "pray walk," as she calls it. It thrills my soul to hear her tiny voice praying for others. During the summer, I sometimes take one or two of the girls along with me. They listen, pray along, and just this fall, my two middle girls have started prayer cards of their own. It sure has sparked some fascinating theological discussion! More importantly, I have found that when something prevents me from going, I miss, really miss that special time with God.

Let your kids overhear your conversations with Jesus. The simplest way to begin is with simple expressions of gratitude and sentence dialog all through the day. As always, most of the values we wish to instill in our children are more caught than taught.

Laying the Foundation—Prayer Starters

+ Whenever you hear a siren, stop and pray for those who are driving the ambulance or police car. Pray for their safety and the health of any who have been ill or might be in an accident. Pray for safe escape for anyone involved in a fire. Pray that they know Jesus. Thank God for the police officers and firefighters who are willing to help keep us safe.

+ When you pass a school building, pray for the teachers and the students who teach and attend there.

+ When you pass a church, pray for the pastors, Sunday school leaders and teachers inside. Pray for the children who go there to grow up to love Jesus.

+ At the grocery store, thank God for the availability of food and the money with which to buy it. Pray for the cashier in your checkout lane.

+ When you pass a park or playground, thank God for beautiful days, strong bodies to run and play, and the gift of fun. Better yet, stop the car to pray, then get out and play!

+ When you pass an ethnic restaurant, pray for the people of that country to come to know Jesus. Pray for the Christians already in that country to grow stronger in their faith.

+ When something happens, for example, a great parking place close to the mall during rain or bad weather opens up, say, "Thank you, God, for providing that place!" If you're walking a distance, say, "Thank you, God, for strong, healthy legs to be able to walk and arms to push this stroller."

+ If you stop for a treat or a drink while you're out running errands, thank God for that too. It doesn't have to be an elaborate meal for us to be thankful.

Your kids will catch on to this idea without you having to lecture. For instance, if I'm distracted while driving and don't hear a siren, Elexa nearly always says, "Mommy! We have to pray for the siren people!"

Great Resources for Kids About Prayer and God

+ *Jesus Must Be Really Special* (Jennie Bishop, Focus on the Family, nd Heritage Builders)—A fun book filled with ideas for parents; the story teaches kids that serving, praying, reading God's Word, and worshipping is a part of real life.

+ *Tuck Me In, God* (Christine Harder Tangvald, Concordia Publishing)—A fill-in-the-blank book with pictures to help children pray about people they have seen in their day, places they've gone, emotions they've felt, things they need to ask forgiveness for, and things for which they're thankful.

+ *I Love My Daddy* and *I Love My Mommy* (both by Scharlotte Rich, Gold 'N' Honey Books)—Charming stories about little kids and their parents including God in ordinary days. Each book contains a story for every season.

+ *I Can Talk To God!* (ages 3 to 5, Focus on the Family and Heritage Builders)—Pull-out bears can be put in little slots while kids talk to God about various situations.

+ *The Adventures of Prayer Bear* (Focus on the Family and Sparrow Communications)—This video features Steve Green and teaches kids that God cares and will answer them when they call on Him.

+ *Little Girls Bible Story Book* and *Little Boys Bible Story Book* (Carolyn Larsen, Baker Book House)—Delightful, simple retellings of classic Bible stories from the Old and New Testaments, each with their own special point to learn. There are baby versions too.

"Impress them on your children...": Daily Rituals

When our littlest girls each came home from the hospital, we allowed the older girls to give the newest arrival a tour of her new home. They delighted in pointing out the nursery, the mobile over the crib, the changing table, the bathtub, and the downstairs family room where she'd get to have family night with the rest of us. We thanked God for this new blessing. Don't just tell your children, show them that God is important to you.

Make sure you are in church. Make it a point to fellowship with other believers. Get each child his or her very own Bible. Help them remember to take it to church with them. There are great toddler Bibles and kid-friendly versions out there. There are even read-the-Bible-through-in-a-year versions for elementary children. Voice your thankfulness that you live in a country where open worship is possible.

An outgrowth of that thankfulness is to acknowledge from whence such blessings came. Each morning, we cart the children around opening the blinds and curtains and asking, "What kind of day did God make today?" The answer is always one of these, depending on the weather: "A cozy, cloudy day!" "A sunny play day!" "A rainy baking day!" "A snowy, fire-in-the-fireplace day!" From the time they were infants the girls then heard us clap and say, "Yeah, God!"

As they grow, the oldest girls teach this to their younger sisters, and they have come to be thankful for more sophisticated things. "Wow! Look at the awesome sunset God made!" "Look, Mom—God rays!" This is Eden's special term for days when white and yellow lights stream down from clouds around the sun. This is exactly how she thinks it will look when Jesus comes back!

Tape a special memory verse to the kids' bathroom mirror or above their beds. On a speaking trip, I purchased pillowcases for each girl printed with various verses about how God guards our rest and keeps us safe. They have been the girls' favorite prize.

Buy or make a set of Scripture cards and laminate them. They're excellent for giving to a child at a particular time of need and for tucking into lunch boxes.

As soon as the oldest two could read, we made a bulletin board with house rules, the books of the Bible, and various verses we thought would be beneficial for them to memorize including John 3:16; the love chapter verses from 1 Corinthians 13; the Beatitudes from Matthew 6; 1 Corinthians 10:13; 1 Timothy 4:12; and others. We didn't make a big deal out of it, just hung it at their level. They pretend to teach school by it and have already started to memorize verses. The oldest two have already learned the books of the Bible. Their Sunday school teachers have reinforced this.

Let your children see you study and read God's Word. When I sit down to do my Bible study, Elexa runs to get an extra Bible and her own tiny Bible study notebook. She gets her own pen and highlighter to mark things in her notebook as we study. Of course she can't read or write, but she is thrilled to listen to some verses I read aloud, turn pages in her own Bible, and write or draw what she thinks was most important that day. I also try to occasionally alternate doing my daily Bible reading at night in each of the girls' rooms. This encourages them to get into the habit with me.

Perhaps you could also write the names of your immediate family members on the back of a bookmark, along with a time slot. As you move through your day, pray for each one at designated times. Let them know what hour they can expect your specific prayers. Recently I ran across one I had used several years ago. It read simply, 9:00 Eden; 10:00 Greg; 11:00 Emmy; 12:00 Ellie. The two that were then in school reported that they would often look at the clock to know when I would be praying specifically for them.

Great Studies for Moms

- *The Power of a Praying Parent,* Stormie Omartian (and the accompanying study guide)—practical praying Scripture for your kids.

- *The Power of a Praying Wife,* Stormie Omartian (and the accompanying study guide)—suggestions for powerful prayers for your husband.

- *15 Minutes Alone with God,* Emilie Barnes—good, brief day-starter.

- *Believing God,* Beth Moore—powerful, in-depth study.

- *31 Days of Prayer for My Teen,* Susan Alexander Yates—focused, specific study for a tough age.

- *The Chocolate Side of Life,* Cindy Sigler Dagnan—study on all aspects of a woman's life: marriage, kids, friendship, time management, self-esteem.

+ Any study resources by MOPS' Elisa Morgan.
+ *In the Eye of the Storm*, Max Lucado—excellent study on how Jesus handled stress.

If you'd like to read Scripture passages out loud to your children, try this: During morning breakfast read the chapter of Proverbs that corresponds with that date. For example, if it's May 9, read the ninth chapter. Solomon's great, practical advice is a terrific jump start on the day.

Do the same with the Psalms at night for yourself or with your husband. If the children read them with you, point out that David asked God for things, questioned God, praised Him, and trusted Him for safety and help. That will be a great book for your kids to refer to all their lives. The Psalms cycle will take you through about five months. I repeat this continuously nearly every year on my own. You begin to memorize effortlessly and key concepts jump out at you on the days you need them most. For a fresh twist, read *The Message* version. It's a great way for the timeless, eternal words to hit home.

"God asks no man whether he will accept
life. That is not the choice. You must
take it. The only choice is how."

Henry Ward Beecher

"Talk about them when you sit at home...when you lie down and when you get up": God in Every Day

Utilize teachable moments. Sometimes the best spiritual lessons can't be planned. They occur when you get to tell a story about something which happened to you as a child. They happen when you are able to praise, correct, or instruct a child after a hard day, an encounter with a difficult playmate, or a time when they were helpful without being asked.

Jesus was a storyteller. He understood that stories stay in our minds. We remember the lesson because it interests us and gives us a visual image. Use whatever relatable objects that are handy. If you're talking about how someone shared Jesus with a friend, take out the salt shaker and recall Jesus' words about how we're salt to the world. Perhaps they could have some salted and unsalted french fries and choose which they prefer.

Or give each child a flashlight. Take them outside and throughout the house, shining it wherever they please. Then herd them into a dark pantry or closet. Point out how much brighter a light shines when it's dark. Explain how we need to be this light to a dark world that doesn't know Jesus.

Incorporate family-night traditions. Choose a few things that you always do. Make popcorn. Order in pizza. Make a dessert together. Make it a fun night, but always include a devotion of some sort.

The Veggie Tales videos are great tools for making devotion time come alive, and at only 30 minutes in length, they'll hold most children's attention. Read the Bible story of each tale and talk about how that applies to you. For example, the video *Are You My Neighbor?* retells the story of the Good Samaritan. Ask if anyone has ever been a good Samaritan to them. Discuss what God meant by neighbor. Talk about people that they might be helpful to, even though they don't get along or don't particularly like them. Explain that we can still love people with *God's* love and show it through actions, even if we don't *feel* like loving them.

The parables and miracles of Jesus are great starting places for devotions from Scripture. Move on to Colossians chapter 3 and Philippians chapter 6 to talk about relationships and getting along with others. Also read Ephesians 6 and 1 Corinthians 13. The book of James is great for discussing how our mouths can get us in trouble!

As the children grow, incorporate a weekly memory verse. Initiate a friendly contest, if you like. My daddy made my sister and me memorize

1 Corinthians 10:13 before we could date. Those words are indelibly inscribed on my heart.

Have a family talent show. Alternate weeks showcasing one child's special talents: singing, playing an instrument, gymnastics, magic tricks. Remind children that all their talents are gifts from God and we can use them to glorify Him no matter what we're doing. If several play instruments, incorporate that into a praise and worship time. Introduce small children to simple choruses like "God Is So Good," "Jesus Loves Me," and "Jesus Loves the Little Children."

Close with prayer. Quick popcorn prayers are good for children. They can say a simple sentence of gratitude or a request. Teach them a simple pneumonic device like ACTS:

+ A—Adoration
+ C—Confession
+ T—Thanksgiving
+ S—Supplication—requests and intercession for others

Don't forget to report and thank God for answered prayers from last week.

Devotional resources for family night.

+ *The Focus on the Family/Heritage Builders Family Night Tool Chest Series* (Jim Weidman, Kurt Bruner, Mike and Amy Nappa, Chariot Victor Publishing)—What makes these books great is they offer tips for accompanying games, activities, and adaptations for families with children of different ages. We only do these types of devotions every four or five family nights, because they take longer and are more involved, but our children really look forward to those devotions and the concepts really stick.

+ *Little Visits With God* and *More Little Visits With God* (Allan

Jahsmann and Martin Simon, Concordia Publishing House)—
Shorter story-like devotions with a central theme and compre-
hension questions good for younger children; a Scripture verse
and then additional Scripture readings provided for older kids.

+ *Sticky Situations* (Betsy Schmitt, Tyndale Kids)—365 short devotions that deal with ethics; Scripture verse and multiple choice
questions that get kids thinking about the right thing to do.

+ *The One Year Book of Devotions for Girls/Boys* (Debbie Bible and
Betty Free, Tyndale Kids)—Based on character principles with
"think about it" questions and accompanying Scriptures.

"And when you walk along the road...": Taking God with You

Unfortunately, it seems that quite a bit of a mom's day is spent in
the car, waiting, chauffeuring, running endless errands. As one wit said,
"It is a mother's duty to deliver her child once obstetrically and by car
forever after." You can chafe at this reality, or you can take advantage of
it. The modern minivan or SUV just might be biblical Jericho's equiva-
lent of the 10-mile sandal walk!

One year, I did my Bible reading in a different way. I purchased the
New Testament on tape and listened to it whenever we were in the car.
Little Ellie would always ask, "Can we put in the Bible music?"

Keep a selection of kid's praise and worship tapes in the car. Choose
contemporary collections of praise choruses, a tape of old hymns, the
Donut Man tapes or the Veggie Tales CDs. Those are fun and teach kids
some great lessons and wonderful old songs.

Word music has even teamed up with various narrators for a series
called *DriveTime Devotions*. Each one is about 2-4 minutes in length.
There are drive-time devotions for moms, dads, and kids. We listen to

one on Monday mornings on the way to school. It's a great, simple way to begin the week.

Be deliberately thoughtful. Let your kids shovel an elderly neighbor's sidewalk. Take trash bags and pick up trash that's blown into your street during a windy trash-pickup day. Offer to get someone's mail or mow their lawn while they're on vacation.

Don't forget God's creation. Leave a little something for the squirrels when it's bitterly cold. Put up a few birdfeeders on the porch or in the yard. Fill a pinecone with peanut butter, roll in birdseed, and hang from tree branches.

Practice thankfulness. During daily errands in the car, play the thankful game. Take turns shouting out things you're thankful for from your house all the way to the grocery store. Or all the way from school to home. Nothing is too silly, too small, or too big.

"Write them on the doorframes of your houses and on your gates...": Proclaiming What You Believe and Sharing God with Others

Save your Christmas cards this year. Place them in a basket and draw one out every week at family night. Pray for that family. If that family is celebrating something, for example, the birth of a new baby, send them a congratulations card. Send a card of encouragement or a sympathy card for a recent loss.

Bundle up on a cold night and put a boxed brownie mix, a copy of your church bulletin, and several packets of instant hot chocolate mix in a cheery gift sack. Go as a family and drop it off to a new family, a shut-in or someone you know is lonely in your neighborhood. Walk, if possible, admire the stars, and thank God for them.

Make a covenant as a family and then make a list of people you can entertain in your home this year. Practice hospitality. Do the adopt-a-leader program, or do the same thing with a lonely college student or a soldier away in a foreign land.

Participate in the Operation Christmas Child program and let your children fill a shoe box full of goodies for a child who has nothing. The several years we did this, our older girls were awed that some children might actually *need* something as basic as a toothbrush. Temporarily humbled, they had a ball choosing a really *cool* toothbrush (Barbie, Spider-man, Dora), pretty hair accessories, new crayons, a coloring book, a beautiful washcloth, and other small trinkets to stuff their shoe boxes.

Pick an ornament from the Salvation Army tree and help fulfill someone's wish. I still remember the elderly woman whose only wish was a pretty flannel nightgown. Eden chose a beautiful one for her. Karen Kingsbury's Red Glove series offers great suggestions of Christmas service projects involving the distribution of red mittens or gloves.

———

In the days of castles and kings, a special flag was flown from the castle turret, proclaiming that the king was in residence. Whether you choose to make a literal flag—or a symbolic one that is evident in your every action—make sure that all those who pass by your home and come in contact with your family know beyond the shadow of a doubt that you serve the One True God and that He dwells with you.

1 Corinthians 13 for Moms

I can read bedtime stories till the cow jumps over the moon and sing "Ten Little Monkeys" until I want to call the doctor—but if I don't have love, I'm as annoying as a ringing phone.

I can chase a naked toddler through the house while cooking dinner and listening to voice mail, I can fix the best cookies and Kool-Aid in the neighborhood, and I can tell a sick child's temperature with one touch of my finger, but if I don't have love, I am nothing.

Love is patient while watching and praying by the front window when it's 30 minutes past curfew. Love is kind when my teen says, "I hate you!" It does not envy the neighbors' swimming pool or their brand-new minivan, but trusts the Lord to provide every need.

Love does not brag when other parents share their disappointments and insecurities and rejoices when other families succeed.

It doesn't boast, even when I've multitasked all day long and my husband can't do more than one thing at a time.

Love is not rude when my spouse innocently asks, "What have you done today?" It is not easily angered, even when my 15-year-old acts like the world revolves around her. It is not self-righteous when I remind my 17-year-old that he's going 83 in a 55-mph-zone, but rejoices in the truth.

Love trusts God to protect our children when we cannot. It perseveres through blue nail polish, burps and other bodily functions, rolled eyes, crossed arms, messy rooms and sleepovers.

Love never fails. But where there are memories of thousands of diaper changes and painful labors, they will fade away. Where there is talking back, it will (eventually) cease. (Please, Lord?) But when we get to heaven, our imperfect parenting will disappear. (Thank You, God!)

When we were children, we needed a parent to love and protect us. Now that we're parents ourselves, we have a heavenly Father who adores, shelters and holds us when we need to cry.

And now these three remain: faith, hope and love. But the greatest of these is love.

QUESTIONS FOR STUDY AND REFLECTION

1. Read 2 Timothy 1:5. Who does Paul think was responsible for Timothy's sincere faith? How do you think they accomplished this?

2. Look at the phrase which follows "sincere faith": "Which first lived in your grandmother Lois and in your mother Eunice." How do *you* live out your faith? Is it evident to your children?

3. What does it mean to you that your influence might ignite a living faith in your children? How do you think this happens?

4. Look at Deuteronomy 6:6-9. Don't just read it from this book, go get your Bible and really look it up and meditate on the words. Which part of God's formula is the easiest for you to incorporate into your home? The most difficult? Why?

5. Look again at question 1. How does knowing that God has entrusted you with a similar charge make you feel? Honored? Overwhelmed? Scared? Inadequate?

6. Deuteronomy 7:9 holds a wonderful promise. God is a faithful God, keeping his covenant to a thousand generations of those who love him. What does this mean to you in light of raising your children to love Him? Thinking back to your parents and grandparents, do you feel as though they passed on a faith to you as God requested? If not, who stepped in the gap for you? Consider that you might also be that person for a child in your neighborhood who does not have a Christian influence.

Action Plan

Choose any of the prayer plans (journal, note cards, list, anything that will get you started) and actively begin praying this week. Begin with baby steps. Trace your children's hands and write the verses and things you wish to pray about inside those tiny outlines. Pray as though their lives depended on it, for they do.

Journal

This week focus on recording answers to your prayers. It is so helpful to have a date, a request, and God's answers written down to refer to on days when prayer doesn't seem to be working. Your journal can become a personal record of God's faithfulness.

Memorize

"Choose for yourselves this day whom you will serve…But as for me and my household, we will serve the Lord" (Joshua 24:15).

Chapter 11

The Marriage Zone: Rediscovering Your Role as Wife

A simple enough pleasure, surely,
to have breakfast alone with one's husband,
but how seldom married people
in the midst of life achieve it.

—Anne Morrow Lindbergh

One of the things that changed for me with astonishing rapidity after the births of my children was the nature of my relationship with my husband. That's not to say I wasn't still madly in love with him, it's just that ever so subtly, my priorities shifted. Poor Greg had a hard time competing with sweet, tiny baby toes, adorable expressions, the demands of nursing and juggling cranky and/or overeager siblings. He had no idea what it was like to entertain one child, snuggle a two-year-old next to me on the couch, and plop the newborn on a Boppy, only to have the two-year-old's jaws open wide behind the unsuspecting infant's head and announce, "Mommy, I really need to bite baby Ellie!"

There were so many changes on top of the sleepless nights, post-baby shock, and the impossibility for a reasonably intelligent, college-educated woman to shower before noon. All these years later, four kids to one of me can still seem like overwhelming odds (until 5:45 PM when Greg gets home). I love my children. I am crazy about them. But I am also crazy about my husband, and I want that to be a mutual and growing situation. From talking to many other women, I know I am not alone in that hope. It's just the "where to start" part that's overwhelming.

No wonder one of the most requested parts of my mommy seminars is the section on marriage. It is sooooo important that we place our marriages above every other earthly priority. And yes, gasp, that has to include our children! Think of it this way. A great marriage serves as a model for your children for their own someday marriages and as the best security blanket. Children blossom under the knowledge that their parents are committed to each other no matter what.

Here is my three-step plan.

Step 1: Glow

We've talked about how our appearance affects our attitudes and our self-esteem, but it's worth mentioning again here, together with our inner-beauty workout. A woman of faith, a woman with a great sense of humor, a woman in tune with God is one gorgeous lady! Pray as you work. Pray a short prayer or breathe a sentence of thanks as soon as you open your eyes in the morning. Remember 1 Peter 3:3-5: "Your beauty should not come from outward adornment...Instead, it should be that of your inner self, the unfading beauty of a gentle and quiet spirit, which is of great worth in God's sight. For this is the way the holy women of the past *who put their hope in God* used to make themselves beautiful" (emphasis mine).

This does not, however, excuse us from expending any effort on our physical appearance. In case you've forgotten, you married a man, who is by nature a *very* visual creature (more on that later). After your time with God, make getting ready physically to meet the day your next priority. Although it's tempting to first load the dishwasher, throw in some laundry, or just hang out, showering, making up, and dressing for the day provides purpose, prevents wasted time, and lessens those unpleasant moments when innocent repairmen and unsuspecting friends drop by and catch us as big-time *Glamour* don'ts. If you don't get dressed at the top of the morning, there's a good chance you'll talk yourself into conserving time by being ready for bed that evening before anyone else.

The easiest thing to toss on in the morning is not necessarily the best. Anticipate your schedule for that day, and dress as nicely as possible. Jeans (Levis, Lee, and Gap jeans offer a variety of fits and lengths; one killer pair is well worth the investment), khakis, and casual jumpers are good and child-friendly alternatives to sweats and jammies. Personally, I am a big fan of overalls. Believe it or not, my favorite pair came from Victoria's Secret and they lasted seven years! (Old Navy has great deals on them, especially children's sizes.) Overalls are cute, fun, comfortable, and practical. The girls and I all have a pair and wear them almost once a week. With a different shirt underneath them, they look different and can go through all seasons.

Looking and feeling put-together is a wonderful mood booster. Knowing this, on really bad days, I won't leave the house, even to feed the dog, without lipstick and earrings. Several girlfriends have adopted my lipstick and earrings minimum standard and now swear that it works.

If it's been a while since your last haircut, go get one. Look through hairstyle books and experiment with what's right for you. Several computer programs and a few websites allow you to "try on" hair in advance to see what you'd look like. Get together with a friend and play beauty shop.

Fix each others' hair and nails and exchange makeup tips. Give your kids plastic curlers or pretend curling irons and let them go at it too.

Eating and Drinking to Shine

It's far too easy to snack more when you're at home. Make healthful eating easier by precutting carrots and celery. Store them in cold water in airtight plastic containers in your fridge. Toss cut-up cauliflower, broccoli, and cherry tomatoes with low-fat Italian dressing; it makes a great lunch with cheese and crackers. Or enjoy veggies with a packet of dry ranch dressing mixed with low-fat sour cream.

Buy fruit and actually eat it. Store washed blueberries, strawberries, seedless grapes, and sliced cantaloupe and watermelon in your refrigerator. Place bananas and washed apples in a basket or glass bowl for a pretty and edible centerpiece.

Ban chips and packaged cookies from your pantry except for special occasions. You can make your own healthier version of chips by thinly slicing sweet potatoes or potatoes and drizzling them with olive oil and kosher salt and baking them in a 400° oven for approximately 20 minutes for an entire pan. When you bake, use whole-wheat flour and brown sugar or honey whenever possible. The better your diet, the more your complexion will glow.

And drink that water! Research tells us that water can keep skin hydrated, plumping up skin, warding off bloating, and flushing impurities. By the time we experience thirst, we are already slightly dehydrated; we can also misinterpret thirst as hunger signals. I'm not a fan of plain water, but a lime or lemon slice provides an inexpensive flavor boost. Many companies also market flavored or vitamin-enriched bottled water.

Exercise and reap the benefits of a healthier body, a healthier self-image, increased energy, and an appreciative husband! The way it makes you feel is well worth the effort. Walk up and down the stairs. (Yep, going upstairs to put away laundry and to monitor fights counts.) Do tummy crunches during commercials and side leg lifts while talking on the phone. Bundle up the kids and walk briskly to the park or around the neighborhood. I have a 25-minute aerobic tape (*Denise Austin's Fat Burning Blast*) that I do three mornings a week during inclement weather. The other two weekdays I do some free-weight lifting. If you have older children, join a YMCA and make exercise a family affair. Walk or work out with a friend or your spouse. If you're accountable to someone, you're more likely to follow through.

Laugh lots! Laughter illuminates and intrigues. Don't you just love to be in the company of someone who can make you laugh? Check out some episodes of *I Love Lucy*, *The Andy Griffith Show*, or *The Dick Van Dyke Show* from your local library. Introduce your kids to some classic entertainment and laugh your abs into rock-hard shape. Or watch an old, perky Doris Day film and lift your spirits while trying to imagine completing your household chores in those outfits—that's always good for a laugh.

Step 2: Grow

Don't let your needs be completely absorbed by the family. Your IQ did not fall into the toy box when you decided to stay home.

Watch enough news programs and read enough headlines to be conversant on current events. Not only does this make you a better citizen at the polls, it also keeps you grounded in the real world. It's very easy to hide at home. That said, don't be obsessive about it either; too much news, especially late at night, tends to make people more sleepless as they worry more.

Be as avid a reader as time can possibly allow. It's amazing what little tidbits of information come in handy at the oddest times. The public library subscribes to many magazines. Check out the newest recipes, fashions, and decorating ideas (even plan a dream vacation!) while your little ones read in the children's section.

Check out a book on tape and listen to it while you carpool and run endless errands. Libraries will often purchase novels or nonfiction books at the patron's request. Our library has purchased nearly every book I've requested, and as an added benefit, the person requesting the book is the first one on the hold list. This is a great way to read the most current books for free; your tax dollars have already paid for it, so take advantage.

If your town has one, browse one of the book superstores that welcome reading and lounging. Check out what's on the bestseller list and what trends are hot. Or, just people watch. Many of those chains have gourmet coffee and dessert shops attached. Splitting a cup of coffee, a scrumptious dessert, and leafing through new books and magazines with your spouse is a great cheap date too!

Step 3: Guard

Neglect is a death blow to marriages. As unromantic as it sounds, your relationship takes work. It must be fiercely protected, tenderly nurtured, and faithfully guarded.

The number-one way to safeguard your marriage is deceptively simple: Acknowledge the fact that *no one's marriage is immune to trouble*. Pretending or hoping that infidelity could never touch our relationships is a luxury we can't afford. Chances are we will be attracted to someone other than our spouse in our marriage. Just being aware of this is a step toward affair-proofing your marriage.

We also really need to be in tune to our partners and learn to anticipate their needs. Unfortunately putting someone else's needs ahead of our own doesn't come naturally. It must be practiced.

Try seeing your husband through another woman's eyes. How does he look? What strengths does he have at work? What qualities does he bring to your relationship? Is he a great help with the children? Can he build almost anything? Does he have a tender heart where you're concerned? Is he a good provider? Purposely focus on these things.

Have a proactive marriage. Since most of us gals were raised on a steady diet of fairy tales, it's disheartening to discover that what comes after the "happily ever after" part is plain old hard work. That sounds so unromantic, but it's time to grow up. There are two equally dangerous myths: Other people's marriages are better than ours, or the really good marriages are easy. Comparisons only serve to breed discontent and promote envy. In reality, all good marriages are the result of effort and tenacious commitment.

When the honeymoon feelings wane and the children begin to arrive, there is a tendency to put marriage on autopilot. Oh, girlfriends, it is so tempting to believe that something which was once effortlessly superb can return to such a state when the kids are grown, but research doesn't bear that out. It used to be that once a couple passed the seven-year mark of marriage, they were good for the long haul. But current divorces are happening around the twentieth to twenty-fifth year of marriage. Why? The empty nest syndrome. Years of talking about nothing but carpool schedules, dentist appointments, permission slips, and work commitments leave a big gaping hole when the last child moves out for college. Husbands and wives discover that they no longer have a foundation to stand upon or to build on.

Date Your Spouse

Getaways are essential. At least once a year, make sure you have an overnight rendezvous. It is unspeakably worth the effort. In theory, I look forward to these with great enthusiasm. In reality, I have a horribly difficult time leaving the children. However, once I'm done crying (usually about ten minutes after we leave), something magical happens. I remember that I am not just somebody's mother, I am also a helpmeet, lover, and friend to this good-looking man sitting next to me. We begin to flirt with each other. We hold hands. We kiss. Our mannerisms and our conversation reflect a genuine desire for each other and delight to be in each other's company. We return, for that precious window of time, to the halcyon days of our courtship, honeymoon, and early years.

Carve out slices of time that are sacred. Sometimes when Greg gets home from work, after the girls are done with their shrieking fest of "Daddy's home! Yeah! Daddy's home!" we'll tell them, "Girls, Mommy and Daddy are going to sit down and visit with each other for just a few minutes. We need to be uninterrupted." We might finish making dinner together or sit on the couch and hold hands, debriefing each other about our respective days. At any rate, it serves as a unifying connector for us.

Put dates with your spouse down on your calendar. Plan them. Why not? You write down everything else that is important. The ideal we shoot for is two date nights a month. Right now though, our budget and time schedules are such that we are committed to one date night a month. We swap child care with another family from church. For five hours they watch our children while we date; on another night, we watch their children for their date. We have found that having those times to look forward to tides us over during the leaner days.

We have fun planning our dates and getaways; often we take turns. Whenever possible, I try to buy a little something new that he's never seen before for date day. I spend extra time on my appearance, even if I'm just going to be wearing jeans. Once my precious children got over the initial shock: "Why are you going to date Dad? Aren't you already married to him?" I explained how important it is for mommies and daddies to remember that they are also best friends and lovers. They love to get in on the action. They might help pick out my jewelry or choose between two potential outfits or help with my hair and makeup. They take great delight in hiding me from Daddy. Often, Greg will stand at the bottom of the stairs and wait for me to appear. The children will squeal, "Don't look yet, Daddy!" And then, "Okay, here she comes!" He makes a big deal of wolf-whistling and catcalling and sometimes even motions for me to spin around. The children giggle, but I hope we're modeling an important practice and good marriage for them.

Connect Spiritually and Emotionally

Pray together. Discuss together. One of my favorite things to do with Greg has been to go through James and Shirley Dobson's devotional books: *Night Light: A Devotional for Couples* and *Night Light for Parents*. We have completed the first book and are halfway through the second. The devotions are short (ten minutes tops, I promise, this is a plus when convincing your guy to do them with you) and provide a launching pad for heartfelt discussions of topics you might not have covered on your own. In my book *The Chocolate Side of Life*, I discuss some important facts about communication and list a series of conversation starters for married couples. These are good during date nights or anytime you want to spice up your conversation.

Connect throughout the day. A goodbye ritual. A phone call. A quick lunch. Can you drop by the office with a surprise picnic basket lunch? A full-body embrace—studies show that this is a proven stress-reducer. Display a few wedding pictures in pretty frames around the house. When you pass them, say a brief prayer for your mate and spend a few moments recalling those romantic feelings. Purchase a stand for your wedding album and look through those pictures every time you dust.

Establish traditions just for the two of you. A special nickname. A specific ritual. Above our bed hangs a wooden sign that reads "Always Kiss Me Goodnight." If one of us forgets, the other is always sure to point up. I always wear my wedding earrings on our anniversary date, even if I am just wearing jeans. We usually watch our wedding video too. It transports us back to those feelings. One couple sets aside the thirtieth of every month (their anniversary date) to meet for lunch, take a walk, go on a date, or send something special to commemorate the commitment they've made.

Boundaries

Greg and I have a general rule not to have lunch alone with a member of the opposite sex. Sometimes, in police work, he has occasionally had to break this rule. For accountability, we've agreed to call each other if this happens. For instance, he might call me and say, "Hi, Babe. If anyone tells you that I had lunch with another woman today, it's true. We drove through McDonald's on our way to another crime scene."

This serves two purposes. First, there's something about human nature that seems to want to gossip. When someone calls to report, I already know. So I can cheerfully say, "I know! They're on their way to a double homicide. Isn't that *romantic?*" That response nearly always kills the rumor mill. Secondly, information shared is in itself accountability. If you ever withhold information from your spouse, that's where the slippery slope begins.

Boundaries are not an expression of mistrust; actually they are an affirmation of the commitment you intend to keep.

Love in Little and Big Ways

I love what Jill Savage, founder of Hearts at Home, tells her audiences: "I have been married for 19 years, 12 of them happily!" It's time for the fun part! How can we make our marriages their very best? Here are some of the favorite suggestions I pass on to women in my seminars:

Preserve some mystery. Surprise him once in a while. Just when he thinks he can predict your reactions, don't say a word when he comes home late and forgets to call first. Share a story about yourself that you haven't yet shared with him. If you're normally a planner, be spontaneous for a change; if you're the fly-by-the-seat-of-your-pants kind of gal, carefully plan an outing.

Encourage him to have an occasional night out with the guys. After all, you've been learning how to grab mommy time. Developing some separate interests keeps things interesting, gives you new things to talk about, and draws you closer.

Read books about marital intimacy. There are two great ones on my must-read list: *Pillow Talk: The Intimate Marriage from A to Z* by Karen Scalf Linamen, and *Is There Really Sex After Kids?* by Jill Savage. A great one for you and your husband to study together is Kevin Leman's *Sex Begins in the Kitchen* or *Sheet Music.*

Practice makes perfect. I'm not sure why, but every time I do a marriage workshop, there are giggles comparable to a class of junior-high kids in biology on reproduction lecture day, when I remind the women that since you are married, you can have sex with your husband and lots of it!

The aforementioned Dr. Kevin Leman writes that after many years of experience in counseling married couples, he is now prepared to tell brides-to-be in their premarriage counseling sessions that if they are not prepared to have sex 2 to 3 times a week with their husbands, they shouldn't get married—it would be committing fraud! During one of our marriage units for the Sunday school class which my husband and I team teach, we assigned them this homework: have sex every single night for a week (yep, weekend included). Having sex can actually increase desire for more sex. I have never heard of a man complaining, "Help, my wife wants me all the time!" A cautionary tale: Some friends of ours, having followed this assignment, blame us for the birth of another child!

Be open and direct about your needs. Sigh. As nice as it would be, expecting our husbands to be mind readers is simply not possible. Remind him that sometimes you just need to be held with no expectation of anything more. That you love long, unexpected, passionate kisses. That flowers are a good thing. That he doesn't have to solve your problems, just listen and share the load.

During crazy times, go ahead and schedule sex. It will be one of the most exciting appointments.

Don't neglect what you wear for the love of your life. Okay, girlfriends, 'fess up. What's your favorite nightie? Is it glamorous satin? Little and lacy? Sensuously silky? Or is it drop-dead flannel? How 'bout that Cowboys T-shirt with the hole under the left arm? I know, I know. What's the point of something unusual? He'll stare at it, drool, and peel it off you in 3.9 seconds. But remember the visual-creature thing? Trust me. He'll appreciate it. Charlie Shedd, in his classic book of marital advice to his daughter, asserts that the family budget shouldn't skimp on two things: good food and lingerie. It's worth the investment. Keep reading the list for more ideas.

Wear a long string of pearls and high heels and nothing else! While we're on this subject, let's just clear something up. In case you've been eyeing your birthday suit and thinking it needs ironing; in case you're the type who tries to drape yourself at bizarre angles hoping for a better body presentation; in case you're the girlfriend who won't ever consider anything other than the missionary position, ever, because at least that way you can suck in your stomach and bury your posterior in the folds of the mattress; let me share with you the result of my informal survey as to what guys really think when they see their wives naked. Are you ready for this? They are thinking, *Wow! I am alone with a naked woman and she is going to let me* *have my way with her! Yowza! Yowza!* So go forth into the bedroom boldly and with confidence. Heck, try a different position too!

Buy your husband a new tie. Fix a dinner just for the two of you late at night and give the tie to him by wearing it and it only.

Slip a hotel key to your husband—if you can arrange it—and have him meet you there for a lunch-hour romp. He'll have a very productive rest of the day.

Rent his dream car—a jeep, a convertible, a Corvette—for a weekend date. Plan on checking out the backseat too.

Impromptu dates. It takes some extra effort, but try surprising your husband by inventing a reason that he needs to meet you somewhere. When he gets there, be all dressed up in your date clothes and go to an impromptu movie or dinner together. At least once in your married life, kidnap him from work on a Friday, have his bag packed and in the car, and get away for the night. One note of caution: Whatever surprises you plan, keep in mind your husband's unique personality. Some husbands may not like surprises…or at least certain kinds of surprises. For example, if you're married to a police officer, you might not want to jump out and surprise him in the dark, even if you are just wearing a trench coat.

Do some housework in nothing but your apron when the kids are away. Don't worry, you won't actually get much accomplished.

Sleep au naturel occasionally. Just keep your robe handy for those inevitable late-night trips to the baby's nursery and toddler's room.

Foundational items. After many moons of heavy-duty nursing bras and grandma panties, I've noticed that *any* matching bra and panty set tends to fan the flames. An added benefit is that even if you've got them on under overalls, you'll still feel desirable and pretty, even if no one else knows they're there.

Put on a racy undergarment or thigh-high stockings. Most lingerie shoppes sell the kind that hold up on their own with an invisible rubber seam at the top; those kinds are far more practical for most of us mommies. Flash him just before you walk out the door to a dinner engagement. I don't really want to get into the issue of thong panties—that's a matter of personal preference. But I will mention, since it's just us girls here, that the new, lacy boy-leg shorts in all kinds of colors can be much more user-friendly and just as sexy.

The best exposure. I'm not sure why, but for some reason, men love garter belts and thigh-high panty hose. If, like me, you're fairly certain that your thighs aren't exactly in the same condition that you recall them to be say, oh, ten years ago (the last time you had the courage to really look), I have good news! Victoria's Secret and JC Penney have both come out with something called a flirt skirt. Instead of being completely exposed, the skirt part (while still tiny) hides upper thighs while the garters peek out from beneath.

Wear something completely different than usual. If you're a pajama top and bottom gal, buy a silky nightgown. If you always wear pink, get something red and sheer, or black and lacy. For a big change, sleep in one of his dress shirts and nothing else.

Try costumes, like a headband with a pair of bunny ears and just your tail to privately celebrate the arrival of spring. A red teddy with features (a crotch that unsnaps) and a Santa Claus hat to ring in the season. Lace cuffs paired with a black teddy. Feed him a snack as his very own private maid. Might you feel silly? Probably...but not for long.

Fishnet stockings are another good bet. You can even wear some of the smaller patterns with a suit for a daytime lunch meeting. It's a detail he'll be sure to notice.

Try buying *him* something sexy for the bedroom. See-through pajama bottoms. Silk boxers.

Variety is the spice of married sex.

+ Gary Smalley says that sexually, men are microwaves, women are Crock-Pots. Tee-hee and amen. Show him the value of a slow simmer this evening!

+ That said, there is also a place for the quickie. Someday, attack him in the laundry room or, if you can get away with it, at his office. Tell him you just can't wait and must have him right now!

+ Try a new location. A private beach. The shower. The guest room. The car—even if it's just in your garage after the kids have gone to sleep. And yes, you may bring the baby monitor with you just to make sure they're still asleep.

+ Call him at work and say, "You. Me. Walk-in closet. 5:30. Naked." Trust me, he'll be there.

+ If you're at home and he's on the phone or working in the garage—and nobody's around—open your shirt and flash him. He's your husband, remember?

+ If you're like me, your bedtime routine probably includes taking off your makeup. Try putting some on—include some bright red lipstick.

+ Take a bubble bath or hot shower together. Surprise him one morning by hopping into the shower with him before work. You'll send your husband off to work a surprised, satisfied man.

+ Lights on? Lights off? It's the big debate for those of us still adjusting to our AC bodies. Try playing an intimate game of strip checkers. The winner gets to choose the lighting! Or buy lots of candles. Candlelight is universally flattering.

Make your bedroom a haven, a respite, a stage for romance. Fresh flowers can be kept in your room for under $5 a week with a grocery-store bouquet. Or fill mason jars with Queen Anne's lace, black-eyed Susans, and daisies from your yard or roadside.

Try a linen spray in vanilla or lavender. Spray your sheets when you fold them down at night.

Make a tape of love songs, a song from your wedding, and your favorite courtship song. Play this softly to mask any private sounds that could be detected by little ears. Get a lock for your bedroom door. Treat him to a lap dance.

Pray that God gives you a heart full of love and desire for your husband. Read the Song of Solomon.

Adjust Your Attitude

We've all heard the classic jokes. "Sometimes I wake up cranky. Sometimes I let her sleep." Or how about the husband who came home from work at the end of a hard day to a crabby wife. In an effort to make things better after a long argument, he says, "Honey, let's back up and pretend I just got home." Obligingly she complains, "It's 7:30 and you're just now getting home?!" As Abraham Lincoln said, "Most folks are about as happy as they make up their minds to be." For the health of your marriage, start making up yours to be happy.

An artist named Martina McBride captured this sentiment in her song called, "Happy Girl." I'm thinking of adopting it as my theme song. The apostle Paul put it this way, "I have learned the secret of being content in every situation." And Solomon, in the book of Proverbs, had some advice for us wives too. "Better a dry crust with peace and quiet that a house full of feasting with strife" (17:1); "Better to live in a desert (or on a corner of the roof) than with a quarrelsome and ill-tempered wife"

(21:19 and 25:24). Yikes! Let that not be us. Here are some more ways to avoid becoming the ill-tempered spouse.

- *Don't ever take him for granted.* Remember that companionship is to men what conversation is to women. Do things with him. Cuddle next to him and watch ESPN. Take turns renting guy movies and chick flicks. Can you talk him into a ballroom dancing class? Read the same book or series together and talk about it while lying in bed with snacks. My husband and I have sometimes read legal thrillers or detective novels together. Read aloud to each other.

- *Dream together.* Find out about each other's secret goals and wishes. Get a home-plan book or some vacation magazines and plan your dream house or ultimate vacation. Be supportive of his goals. He's sure to return the favor.

- *Reread some of the love notes and cards you wrote during courtship* to rekindle the flames. Then, write him a new one. Send him a card or surprise at work—with caution. I have shared some of my humiliating tales in other books.

"You are my unutterable blessing…I am in full sunshine now"—Robert Browning.

Try whispering in your sweetheart's left ear. According to a *Woman's World* (May 2004) article, Sam Houston State University researchers have discovered that emotional requests are better understood when they're spoken into the left ear. That's the side controlled by the right brain where emotional and creative stimuli are processed.

- *Shave your legs. Hold hands as you drift off to sleep.* Let him know you appreciate how hard he works to provide for your family.

Agree to take turns sleeping in, getting up with the baby, or entertaining the kids.

+ *Pray for him.* I mean it. Don't just say it, actually spend time thanking God for your husband. Ask for His watch and care over him during the day. Pray for God's hand on your marriage. That He would keep your husband's thoughts pure and his desire for you only.

+ *Fantasize about him while he's away.* Look at him again through the eyes of your dating self. Remember why you fell in love with him. Look into his eyes when he talks. Give him your full attention. Notice that cute, lopsided grin he has when he's recounting an amusing part of his day.

+ *Cut out phrases and pictures from magazines* and use them to make him a card or a story. I did this once with the story of our courtship. He still keeps it in the top drawer of his dresser.

+ *Make it a point to be familiar with your husband's job.* What does he do all day? What unique stresses does he encounter? If it's ever possible, spend a day, or part of one, at work with him, just as a quiet observer. I have been on police ride-alongs with my husband. I listened to him give a tour of the Children's Center— a child-advocacy center which allows victims of child abuse to tell their story in a safe atmosphere with all law enforcement professionals on-site—as though I were just another citizen. I got sitters so I could go watch closing arguments of some of the trials which he'd prepared as investigator for the prosecuting attorney. Seeing the career side of your husband is an eye-opener. You'll appreciate him so much more and understand him much more fully.*

---

* A special note for all the law-enforcement wives who ask me questions about their special circumstances. The book I always refer to is called *I Love a Cop: What Police Families Need to Know* by Ellen Kirschman, Ph.D. (Guilford Press).

My daddy once mailed me a newspaper clipping that was found among my Grandmother Eva's things. It's an undated and unmarked piece by Ruth Millett from a Springfield, Missouri, newspaper. If I had to guess, I'd say it was written in the late '40s. The advice is timeless.

We Women

What every woman doesn't know:

That even though her husband claims he never wants her to change,
he would be the first to grow bored with her
if she didn't keep on growing
and changing and becoming more of a person through the years.

That a wife can keep her husband closer to her through the years
by giving him as much freedom as he wants rather than
by trying to keep him constantly at her side.

That boredom is the worst threat to marriage. The wife who
keeps things humming is doing a lot to keep a husband.

That even though a man knows nothing about feminine fashions,
he knows when his wife looks well-groomed
and attractive. So her efforts
to look her best aren't wasted on him
even though she occasionally gets
complimented on a "new dress" she has had for three years.

That most men are happier playing host than guest. The wife
whose husband never wants to go anywhere can be made
more sociable by plenty of entertaining at home.

That nothing does more for a man's contentment than the sound
of a woman's laughter. The more a wife finds to laugh about
good-naturedly, the happier her marriage will be.

*That taking care of the details of family living and straightening out
minor crises are a woman's responsibility. The less she worries
her husband about small matters the better.*

*That tears quickly lose their effectiveness if often resorted to.
It is easier for a man to run from a woman's tears
than to cope with them.*

*That no victory won by nagging is worth the price—
which is being regarded as a nagger by the man who gives in.*

*Not every woman knows these facts about men and marriage.
But lucky are the ones who do.*

———

Somehow I feel a kinship with my Grandma Eva, although she died when I was six months old. I know that several generations back, the women in my family were doing their part to last 'til death do us part. My own mother left me the same legacy. Although my precious daddy died of cancer at age 56, Mother and Daddy had been married for 34 years, 1 month, 12 days, 8 hours, and some-odd minutes. I'll never forget.

Proverbs 4:23 reminds us, "Above all else, guard your heart, for it is the wellspring of life." Carefully screen what you allow in that special place. Pay attention when it seems your thoughts drift to someone else who might appreciate your work at home more than your husband does. Don't watch anything that makes you become critical of your marriage.

I must confess I love a good romance novel.
Oh, I don't like smut novels, but I *adore* good old-
fashioned romance. Why am I mentioning this?
Because characters dreamed up in a writer's mind

don't have to meet the cold reality of life, they can foster discontent. How can our husbands hope to compete with a fictional dream man who fills his beloved's apartment with roses and remembers the anniversary of the first time he saw her? If reading them means I can't appreciate the spontaneous bouquet of wildflowers Greg may bring me from the front of our house, then I need to avoid them. Make your choices carefully.

Christian fiction houses are finally allowing writers to craft real-world situations and characters and the results are great reads. Some of my favorite suggested fiction books and authors: Karen Kingsbury—check out the 5-volume Redemption series which she is cowriting with Gary Smalley; the Seasons series by Terri Blackstock and Beverly LaHaye; Francine Rivers; Catherine Palmer; Jan Karon's Mitford series is delightfully uplifting; Jamie Langston Turner (a new favorite); Dee Henderson's realistic military and police-profession oriented romantic thrillers. Each month I will have new suggested readings for moms on my website.

In her book *Pillow Talk*, Karen Linamen has this to say about unrealistic expectations: It isn't true that "the rest of the world is enjoying romance and wild passion while we're spending Saturday night replacing the baking soda in the refrigerator. The realities are these: There are no perfect men. No perfect marriages. No perfect love lives. So let's stop pretending there are. Until we do...we may never have a real shot at contentment and happiness with what we've got—real life."

The wise King Solomon, who had experience with a vast number of wives, counseled husbands to "rejoice in the wife of their youth." Girlfriends, make sure your husband has plenty of reasons for rejoicing!

As I wrap up this chapter, I am freshly returned from an overnight getaway with my husband. A quaint bed-and-breakfast with glorious country scenery. Red barns, chunky bleached hay bales standing like oversized wigs on fresh-mown green fields. A charming and scrumptious breakfast. A cozy feather bed. A Jacuzzi. Candlelight. There was time for swimming, lounging in the sun, reading good books, having great conversation, and even flirting. We enjoyed dinner out at a restaurant that didn't serve french fries, as well as hand-holding, and tender glances.

Another block cemented in the foundation of our commitment to each other. In good times. In tough times. At all times. Forever.

QUESTIONS FOR STUDY AND REFLECTION

1. Do you think fairy tales and Hollywood screen versions of marriage have affected your expectations of what marriage should look like? What is the best thing about marriage in your opinion? The most difficult?

2. Do you have a secret list of things you're hoping your spouse will change? Pray about them. Ask God to begin change with you. Write down the list and tear it up, surrendering everything to God.

3. Look up the following scriptures. After each one, jot down the central thought God must have about marriage.

   Genesis 2:18

   Malachi 2:16

   1 Peter 3:1

   Proverbs 18:22

   1 Corinthians 7:3-5

   Deuteronomy 5:21

   Genesis 24:67

   Colossians 3:18

4. With which of the above key concepts do you struggle most in your marriage? Submission? Faithfulness? The marriage bed? The example? Being a completer?

   Why do you think it is so difficult for you?

5. What example did your parents' marriage model for you? How has it affected your marriage? What Scripture could you find to affirm a good model or to correct a poor one?

Action Plan

1. Plan a date with your spouse for this month. Surprise him by wearing your hair a new way, a new outfit, a manicure or some sexy underwear, different from your usual choice. Your goal is for him to think, "Wow!"

2. Initiate sex with your husband at least once this week. Pray in advance that your whole being—body, mind, emotions, and soul—will participate with you.

3. Keep a list of your husband's wishes. Jot down a book he mentions he'd like to have or that he'd like to go to a major-league baseball game this year. Work on making a few of them come true!

Journal

Write a comparison/contrast paragraph about your marriage as it was during your first year and as it is now. Notice any changes, good or bad, and write observations of what things you could change, have changed for the better, or some old traditions you could reinstate.

Memorize

"Her husband has full confidence in her and lacks nothing of value. She brings him good, not harm, all the days of her life" (Proverbs 31:11-12).

Chapter 12

Unfaithful Lessons

Together we have loved, laughed,
sacrificed and endured.
I would not change a thing.

—*Unknown*

"They'd been married for 25 years." "Can you believe he asked her for the 'D' word over a bouquet of roses and dinner?" "And I hear the other woman was only 23 and not even that attractive!" "Wonder what went wrong. I wonder if it could ever happen to us?"

It seems you can hardly have a conversation these days without someone broaching the subject of unfaithfulness. We talk about people we know who are going through it. Then we worry, alone or with our best friends, about the possibility of unfaithfulness touching our own relationships.

Popular movies like *The Bridges of Madison County* and *The Horse Whisperer* have become affair classics, exploring the temptation of infidelity and the subsequent fallout. So-called reality shows like *Temptation Island*, deliberately test a couple's commitment to each other by throwing them into romantic settings and situations with others. The nighttime drama *Desperate Housewives* seems to have incorporated unfaithfulness as a central theme. Hollywood manages to make having an affair border on glamorous. But the reality is that adultery is ugly. Lives touched by it are never the same. When unfaithfulness occurs, it affects all of us. We take a hard look at our own marriages, or at least we should, for there are significant lessons to be learned.

Aside from what we discussed in the last chapter, what else can we do? Don't take each other for granted. We know this rule and yet we all break it. Romantic intentions get buried under the drudge of daily living. *You forgot to pick up the dry cleaning. Whose turn is it to take the kids to soccer practice? You're going to make us late again!* Hardly the stuff of mind-blowing passion. Yet people don't just wake up one morning and say, "I think I'll cheat on my spouse today." Instead, relationships are slowly undermined by a rather innocuous term—marital drift. It is the leading cause of divorce.

Drifting sounds painless. Pleasant even. I can almost hear the soft slapping of the waves against the boat. Feel the sun kissing water-drenched skin, warming my hair. But drifting, by definition, means there is no set course. You're going nowhere. The boat stagnates; the course is eroded by the drip, drip, drip of juggling jobs, kids, electric bills, school, and church obligations and chores.

In an ongoing special report series entitled "The State of the Union," *Ladies' Home Journal* talked with several marriage experts and reported that strong marriages have a ratio of at least five positive interactions for each negative one.[1] Dr. Gary Smalley, Christian relationship expert, calls these positive interactions making deposits in the love bank. If you are constantly degrading, ignoring, disrespecting your husband and your oneness, you *will* end up overdrawn—and the fees are hefty!

For type A's, problems can arise as a result of our exacting standards, fairy tales notwithstanding. Ruth Bell Graham, wife of evangelist Billy

Graham, wrote, "It is a foolish woman who expects her husband to be to her that which only Jesus Christ Himself can be." And while we know this, it is tempting to succumb to the notion that the right man could solve our dissatisfaction. Wrong. In fact, "the conviction that a marriage must be perfect makes a marriage fragile."[2] Fragility equals vulnerability.

Setting the Tone

Homecomings are very important. Studies show that the first seven minutes after you arrive home set the tone for the entire evening. I don't know about you, but even *I* can behave for that long! Try this simple exercise: Meet each other at the door at the end of the day and kiss. Not just a peck, but a courtship kiss. I don't always succeed, but I do make a concerted effort to squirt on perfume and reapply some lipstick around the time that I expect Greg home. Sometimes I even have a cold glass of iced tea or lemonade or a mug of cocoa waiting for him. I know it seems hopelessly old-fashioned, but I am determined to do my part in making him a happy man at home. Make those first minutes pleasant and conflict free. Tempting as it is, this is not the time to throw the children at him and bolt or to present him with a list of gripes/bills/things that are broken.

"Reflect upon your present blessings—of which every man has many—not on your past misfortunes, of which all men have some."

—Charles Dickens

It is so easy to fall into the trap of playing insidious games like "Who had the worst day?" or "I do far more around here than you do." Don't play. We have the potential to be alarmingly effective drippers, naggers, and complainers. If we don't keep our words in check, we may end up being like the wife in this story our preacher told:

> A man once went to Rabbi in a rather alarmed state. "Help me, my wife is trying to poison me!"
>
> "Oh, no—that can't be," the Rabbi replied. "You simply must have misunderstood. I'll talk to her and get back with you."
>
> A week later the Rabbi called the man on the telephone. "I spoke with your wife on the phone for three hours. Wanna know my advice? Take the poison!"

Joking aside, I don't want you to misunderstand. It is not solely your responsibility to make this marriage work. Submissiveness does not equal being a doormat with W-E-L-C-O-M-E tattooed across your stomach. I am saying that while marriage takes tenacious commitment and two partners who are willing to go the distance, we as wives should do everything in our power to make our marriage a great place to be and to stay. Then, surrender the rest to God.

When unfaithfulness happens around you, make it a springboard for discussion and a catalyst for drawing you closer. Ideally, you and your spouse should explore attitudes about unfaithfulness before situations arise. Talk about your expectations of marriage and your needs.

My preacher friend, Sherm, put it this way: "I realized it was even more important for me to be open with my wife after some friends of ours split up. I forced myself to share more emotionally. And although we didn't plan it, when we climb into bed at night now, one or both of us will turn to the other and say, 'I've been faithful to you today.' That simple statement makes me conscious of my commitment."

Take heart though, according to John Gottmann, author of *The Seven Principles for Making Marriage Work*, studies also show that "among the most divorce-proof marriages are those with a breadwinner husband and a stay-at-home wife." Obviously there are many factors which make that true, and certainly it isn't guaranteed without our efforts and God's hand; however, it's nice to add another thing in the plus column for being at home!

Reading the Barometer

We've already talked at length about our husbands' sexual needs in the previous chapter; however, let me make one more point here. While sex is not even close to half the health of a marriage, it is usually an accurate barometer of how the rest of the relationship is going. In every marriage, sex is important.

Perhaps one of the most eye-opening, life-changing things I ever learned about married sex was this concept: Taking care of your man's sexual needs on Friday night does not buy you any offtime for the rest of the week. I read this and was just floored. Flabbergasted. While I truly enjoy intimacy with my husband and considered myself well-read and informed on such subjects, I found I had been guilty of just such beliefs. *I am absolutely exhausted. Since we had such a great time in bed last night, he probably won't need any more until...Wednesday.*

Wrong. A man is wired so that he could actually want more sex in oh, say, an hour! Certainly by the next day. And what will it take to spark this desire? Anything from catching a glimpse of you as you put on or take off your bra to the sight of you in a towel fresh from the shower, or a slight glimpse of cleavage as you unload green peppers into the vegetable bin. In short, just about everything. All of us would be wise to remember this and whenever possible be warm, willing participants. Again, I am not excusing husbands who use dissatisfaction in the bedroom as rationalization for unfaithfulness. However, we need to fulfill and sate our husband's sexual needs so they have one less temptation.

Pray actively and specifically for your marriage. My friend Vickie and I have developed a two-prong prayer that we pray over our marriages. One part came from our heart's desires and the other from a Beth Moore Bible study that we took together: *Lord, please make me ever more attractive in my husband's eyes. Make me sensitive to his needs and supportive of his dreams. In our bedroom, may I thrill to his touch. Amen.*

I have also prayed the second part of that prayer for friends that have been the victims of childhood sexual abuse. Intimacy can be such a struggle for any precious soul who has had to endure such an abuse of trust. If you are in that situation, I urge you to find help with a godly, professional counselor. Don't miss out on God's gift to you as a married woman: a healthy, fulfilling sex life.

Safeguard Your Relationship

Develop an accountability system. Sadly, infidelity is not just a male phenomenon anymore, if it ever was. More and more women are having affairs. You need to be accountable to each other, to a trustworthy, believing, same-sex friend, and to God. Cultivate a trustworthy friend with whom you can discuss that fleeting attraction you have to a co-worker, a fellow committee member, a church friend. Verbalizing it takes some of the mystery and power away. Plus you have a prayer partner committed to keeping you accountable about your feelings and actions. Whatever you do, do *not* verbalize your attraction to that person. It will not help, it will not "get it out of the way," it will not make your relationship safer.

If Internet porn is a male problem, chat rooms and emotional affairs are a huge problem for women. I'm going to say a hard thing here, precious girlfriends. The world would have you believe that as long as your online relationship (or thought life or correspondence) isn't consummated, you're not really cheating. In fact, I have seen magazine articles that tout the benefits of "harmless flirting." Here is truth: *Anything* that takes time and energy away from that which should be spent preserving your number one earthly priority—your marriage—is cheating!

I shared this in a workshop with a group of 500 women at a conference last year. One precious woman waited for me until all the people I was talking to had gone. With tears streaming down her face, she grabbed both my hands and in an anguished whisper confessed, "How did you know? I'm the one with an online friend. I told myself it didn't mean anything. My husband is gone so much and I'm just so lonely. But I really needed to hear that, and I'm going to try some of the things you talked about today in my marriage." How my heart breaks for her. I hugged her and prayed with her. It could have been any one of us; who among us hasn't felt lonely?

Keep your computer in an open area. One couple, whenever possible, has made a commitment to go to bed at the same time. If he has a project, she stays up and reads with him. If she can't sleep, he keeps her company. If you feel the need to hide certain phone calls, e-mails, or business lunches from your spouse, red flags are not only flying everywhere, they're smacking you in the face!

My husband and I have made a pact to be transparent about all activities involving members of the opposite sex. Strive to be above reproach in everything you do.

Did You Know?

- Recent polls conducted by the University of Chicago show that around 25 percent of men and 12 percent of women have been unfaithful.
- The number-one affair partner is a co-worker.
- Warning signs of an affair include unexplained absences, a sudden change in personality, dress, weight, or sexual patterns.
- Who's vulnerable? Well, anyone, but statistically the odds increase if you have recently experienced a major life change (job responsibilities increase or decrease dramatically; birth or loss of a child; change of residence; loss of a loved one), if your parents were unfaithful, or if you keep company with friends who are habitually unfaithful.
- "Swinging"—that is, swapping partners at parties or on couples' vacations—is on the rise again, even among Christian couples, who rationalize that God wants them to

"help" the other couple or that they're simply rejuvenating their own relationship. Isn't Satan clever?
- Affairs are likely to reoccur unless the root problems that sparked them are addressed.[3]

Costly Decisions

Emily Brown, author of *Affairs*, writes, "With affairs, boundary drift is always part of the picture." Boundary violations include arriving home late without a phone call, fudging about the price you paid for an item, or hiding certain information from your spouse. If you're not careful, you will begin to justify the violations, and they gradually grow larger. I have a feeling that's why Jesus asked us to be faithful in the small things. "It takes only a second to destroy trust in a marriage; it takes a lifetime to preserve," recounts Kathie Lee Gifford, in an interview after husband Frank's highly publicized affair.[4]

Unfaithfulness is costly. It's worth preventing. A recent news program featured a classic infidelity triangle: the husband, the wife, and the husband's secretary. What made this case so unusual is that the ex-wife sued the secretary for luring her husband into an affair and a North Carolina jury awarded her a whopping $1 million!

Affairs always involve consequences. David and Bathsheba's sin cost them the life of their firstborn. Even after forgiveness, the consequences hang around: a tarnished reputation, possible STDs, unwanted pregnancy, children who are forced to deal with the fallout of divorce, loss of trust between you and your spouse.

Don't kid yourself. People are watching your marriage, including your children, your co-workers, fellow PTA members, your church family, and those loved ones who watched you make those binding vows.

Non-Christians observe us to see if having Christ in our marriages really makes a difference.

I was dusting a shelf in our bedroom this morning, and I picked up a doll that rests there, a bittersweet memento of my childhood. She was the very first china doll I ever got; my mother had finally decided I was responsible enough. She cautioned me though, not to take it to school. One day I ignored her. The doll fell off of my desk and her head shattered into eight pieces. I am forever indebted to a girl that I wasn't that good of friends with; while I bawled, she picked up those pieces and carefully glued them back together with amber school glue. When the glue dried and I retied the bonnet, you hardly noticed the cracks, but they're still there. And if you slide the bonnet back, well, there's a inch long section of a china head that's missing. She's fixed. She's useable, but the scars are still there.

The same is true of adultery. It's devastating, shattering. A world gets blown to pieces. Long after forgiveness has been received or given, rebuilding trust remains an issue. But by God's grace, it can be repaired. Greg and I have friends who have been remarried—to each other—after unfaithfulness! We know others who are struggling to repair their trust and limping along together, slowly but surely. Healed but with scars.

We would be wise to consider the cost in advance. Make a list of all the people you'd have to tell about your unfaithfulness. Picture their faces; picture their pain. Your husband. Your children. Your parents. Your dearest friend. Those in your prayer group. Seek God's face. See Him? His eyes are flooded with tears.

Unfaithfulness reminds us of our human frailty and draws us back to God. And that is a good thing, for that is where marriage began.

"What God has joined together, let man not separate" (Jesus, in Matthew 19:6).

QUESTIONS FOR STUDY AND REFLECTION

1. Has there ever been a time in which you were attracted to someone other than your spouse? If so, what circumstances made that possible? How did your thoughts and actions contribute to that vulnerability? If not, what do you suppose your response would be to such a situation?

2. In light of Matthew 5:28-29, are there any television shows or books which cause you to fixate on an ideal or person which is unhealthy for your marriage?

3. Read Proverbs 14:1. How do you think this verse could apply to infidelity? Do you ever think that straying is the fault of only one partner? Why or why not?

4. Read Proverbs 12:22. Are you guilty of any of the boundary violations discussed in this chapter? Confess them to God right now.

5. Read Proverbs 6:32. In what way does adultery destroy the person who is unfaithful? Have you personally witnessed such results? Write the initials down of any couple for whom you might need to pray. Do it.

6. In this chapter we learned that expecting perfection in marriage makes a marriage vulnerable. Have you been guilty of demanding or secretly wishing for perfection in your marriage? Of comparing your marriage to someone else's? How is it affecting your attitude? Your marriage?

7. Read Proverbs 15:22. Do you have in place an older, godly couple who could mentor you? A godly, same-sex friend to whom you could be transparent and accountable regarding matters of the heart? Make a list of possibilities and pray that God would show you how to choose wisely.

Action Plan

Go somewhere on neutral territory for coffee or a Coke this week with your husband. Discuss some of the issues and perhaps even set up boundaries for your marriage with which you both feel comfortable. Reaffirm your commitment to faithfulness.

Make a small collage of advertisements and magazine pictures depicting couples. Are any realistic? Which ones foster comparison or discontent? Now make a list of at least ten qualities you appreciate about your husband. Consider sharing the list or actively praising him for those things this week.

Journal

Write a specific prayer asking God to safeguard your marriage, your thoughts, your actions, your home. Use as many details as you can. At least once a week, open to this prayer and pray it over your spouse.

If unfaithfulness has touched your marriage, pray that you can forgive or be forgiven. Pray that God would heal and restore trust. If it has not, invoke His protection.

Memorize

"A man's ways are in full view of the Lord, and he examines all his paths" (Proverbs 5:21).

Chapter 13

Joy and the Tinkertoys

Homekeeping hearts are happiest.
—*Henry Wadsworth Longfellow*

I would love to tell you all about the hidden glamour of being a mother. I would love to tell you that I am finishing this chapter on a brand-spanking-new laptop computer at a quaint rolltop desk with a view of majestic mountains, capped with white party hats and shaded in hues of lavender, smoke, and dusky purple. I am borrowing a wealthy friend's log-hewn cabin and the last of my writing time has been spent surrounded by décor and ambiance worthy of the glossy pages of *Country Home* magazine. Real, live amber waves of grain are applauding the fact we're nearing the end of this literary journey of lessons—this time of life and home improvement. A lone bald eagle circles a towering pine. I can almost smell the fragrance, it's so green. This vista unfolds before me like an impossibly gorgeous, custom-made mural, cut to fit an enormous bay window with custom beveled panels.

Regrettably, I must confess that the picture above is only in my mind (told you I had quite the imagination!). Here's the reality that you might actually buy: I don't know any wealthy friends with cabins—they're all semiyoung, mostly broke mothers like me. It's a cold, dreary January day, and the rain is coming down in sheets. The load of towels in the dryer is clanking (yes, clanking!) causing me to wonder if I ought to get up and go see what the children have added besides laundry. The little I can see out my office window is hampered by a set of dusty wooden blinds, the bulk of an eight-year-old computer, and other assorted paraphernalia that come from meeting a deadline. Instead of the bald eagle screeching majestically (or whatever it is they do), the only noises I hear (besides the dryer) are the spin cycle on the washing machine and the loud waterfall from the dishwasher on the outside wall of my office. In about three minutes, my kitchen timer will ding, and then I will go upstairs and carry a grumpy toddler out of a cozy bed and buckle car seat buckles on the way to pick up my oldest girls from school. We will proceed from there to get their hair trimmed (yep, all of them). Oh joy!

Actually, in a demented mother sort of way, it will be joyful. Okay, the only mountains you may see in your day are mounds of laundry and hills of dust bunnies, but there is joy and humor to be found almost anywhere. Just think what you might be missing if you weren't staying home. Like what, you ask? Let me give you some personal examples and then chuckle along as you recall your own.

When Emmy was two, her favorite song was "Lello Shine" (that's "This Little Light of Mine, I'm Gonna Lello Shine," for the uninitiated). While we were driving into town to do errands, she requested that we sing all the verses. And when you have to entertain children for a 20-minute drive, you give in. I obliged, doing the motions with my right hand, driving with the other and singing with wild abandon. Apparently another driver took it the wrong way. There goes *my* witness. I got so tickled that I swerved and thought the policemen hidden in the parking lot of the elementary school might stop me for drunk driving!

How else would I have seen my two-year-olds earnestly press baby dolls to their belly buttons so they could "nurse"? I'd have missed the infinite sweetness of scooping up my babies anytime from wherever they were resting—floor, nursing Boppy pillow, baby swing, cradle, kitchen table, snug in their carriers—to receive a slobbery kiss or to curl myself around their tiny sleeping forms for a few stolen moments during the day.

I wouldn't be trailed by a small band of admirers who want to assist with dusting, ride the vacuum cleaner, or unfold "lashclothses." I wouldn't be able to drop everything if a tiny voice inquired, "Mommy, could you read thisa booooook?" I'd have missed my Ellie's first wide open, toothless grin.

I might have been busy grading papers in my classroom when Eden ran down the lane crying, "No one played with me on the playground today! That hurt my feelings!" Instead, I rocked her in my arms, and we ate a bit of cookie dough.

I might have missed Emmy's first steps or her "concerts," which all began "Jesus loves the little childreeen!" and ended "Cha-cha-cha!"

Three-year-old Elexa and I were wrapping Christmas presents in front of a roaring fire. I was feeling rather sentimental and so I told her she could choose the wrapping paper for her daddy's present. She pointed at a roll of Blue's Clues paper. "Silly girl"—I squeezed her—"that's for birthdays. I meant you can choose any Christmas paper!" She giggled and so I began pressing kisses all over her sweet little face and chanting, "Silly, baby girl. You're mommy's crazy girl. Blue's Clues paper...silly little one." She wriggled away and pointed a finger at me. "Better not talk like that about me or I will have *big* problems when I grow up!" I thought I'd die laughing!

You can try to plan fun, but often it's the little things that are most fun and the ordinary situations that tickle the funny bone best. I read this example ages ago in *Reader's Digest*. I clipped it and put it in my journal so I could laugh again and again.

> *While on maternity leave, a woman from our office brought in her*
> *new bundle of joy. She also had her seven-year-old son with her.*
> *Everyone gathered around the baby, and the little boy asked,*
> *"Mommy, can I have some money to buy a soda?"*
> *"What do you say?" she said.*
> *Respectfully, the boy replied, "You're thin and beautiful."*
> *The woman reached in her purse and gave her son the money.*
> —Submitted by M. Nickse, Connecticut

Undoubtedly there are some days that you and I will wonder if our choice to be primarily homemakers is making a difference. Will our children even remember the hours of rocking, countless stories, endless walks, routines, traditions, and daily life? Or will it just be comfort for us while we're reduced to having wheelchair races down the halls of our local nursing homes? I assure you, every day, each situation, regardless of how ordinary, how broken, how daily, is a blank canvas. An opportunity for imprinting a memory, a lesson, a value on impressionable little minds. Open each day like a present, knowing it may become anything you want.

It was a hectic day. I was grumpy, stuck in the house on a cold day with a toddler who didn't feel like napping and a deadline looming. The doorbell rang and I answered it. A 79-year-old man stood there. "Got your wood."

"Oh!" was my quick and surprised reply; I certainly didn't know that anyone of his estimable age still cut and delivered firewood. "How are you?" "Cold!" He grinned. Elexa and I put on our coat and mittens and went outside to help stack wood.

As we stacked, we visited. Actually, he told me his life story, and I listened. He had been a member of the Eighty-Second Airborne Division during World War II. He and his wife married young, started with nothing, and saved like crazy. They built their own home. They had three children; one son was killed in Vietnam. They're retired now, getting ready to celebrate their sixtieth wedding anniversary!"Oooh," I breathed, "that's so wonderful! That's what I want. I want a sixtieth anniversary." He grinned that charming grin. "Nah! When you get there, you'll want to keep going. Shoot. We're going for our seventieth!" We finished with the wood. I offered to send him off with a mug of homemade cocoa. "Thank you kindly," he answered, endearing with his old-fashioned phrases, "but I must've drunk a gallon of coffee before coming over here."

"Well," I turned to Elexa, "we'll tell your sisters that we met a real life hero today!" He laughed. "Talk me up big, wouldya?" I assured him I would. What a find in the midst of ordinary.

During our weekly jaunt to the library, Emmy chose a Winnie the Pooh story. You might remember it from your own childhood. Pooh and Piglet discover that it's Eeyore's birthday. Pooh decides to take him a pot filled with "hunny." Piglet races home to get him a balloon. On the way to Eeyore's house, Pooh experiences a rumbling in his tummy and eats all the honey in the pot. Piglet trips, falls, and pops the balloon. They present their sorry gifts to Eeyore. In an uncharacteristic burst of optimism, Eeyore exclaims, "Oh, it's a useful pot. I can put things in it!" And into the pot went the deflated piece of rubber balloon. I love that story. Joy? It's really all in the perspective. Who knows how many broken situations are really just "useful pots" waiting to happen.

Emilie Barnes, in her book *Home Warming*, inspired me with the tale of the wonderful tea party she gave her granddaughter Christine on the occasion of her thirteenth birthday. While planning for the event,

Emilie kept an eye out at garage sales and antique stores for old teacups and saucers. At the tea party, each girl was given a different tea cup, a lace hankie, and a small silver spoon.

After the party she washed and dried all the cups and gave them back to the girls. Emilie asked each one to look at her own cup. Each one different, beautiful, useful, just like the girls. Examine your teacup, she urged them. It might have a chip or a crack. But it is still beautiful and useful. In your lives, you may experience the crack of rejection by a college or a boyfriend. You might become chipped as life unfolds. But you will be like these teacups, still beautiful and still useful. Each girl got to carry home her teacup, hankie, and spoon as a reminder of the lesson of worth they learned on that day.

I want you to finish this book feeling affirmed in your chosen life's work as a wife and mother. And let's be creative as we remind our children and our mate of their incredible worth to God.

> The value of jobs handled by a stay-at-home parent would cost approximately $70,000 per year (U.S. Department of Labor, cited in a recent insurance advertisement). That's just for five 8-hour days, including child care, house maintenance, cooking, and carpooling! Woo hoo!

Recognizing Joy

Remember the opening scene from *The Sound of Music?* Maria has wandered away from the abbey because life is simply too joyous not to answer the call of the mountains. Life beckons to her. She throws open her arms and twirls around in pure, unabashed joy. I used to be more like that. I made neighborhood children play *Sound of Music* with me. I even had the privilege of playing the part of Maria in a Little Theatre production. I lived the dream; I'd like to be more like that again.

Joy may not always be so exuberant. It can take different forms at different times. Joy can be contentment. Joy can be delight. Joy can be elation. Joy can be mirth. Joy can be celebration. But joy is always infectious, and joy always begins with a thankful heart. Since your family will most often absorb your moods and adopt your outlook, why not strive for an attitude of gratitude?

Talk show host Larry King once collaborated with Rabbi Irwin Katsof on an article compiling various thoughts about prayer and its relationship to gratitude. I loved this insight from that article in a quote by Dennis Prager:

> My realization is that the most important component of happiness, by far (there isn't a close second), is gratitude. Prayer is a major vehicle to gratitude. Nothing instills it as much as religion and prayer done correctly. Not request prayer, but grateful prayer. Thank you, God. My favorite holiday is Thanksgiving. The day of gratitude to God.[1]

I have much to be thankful for. Much to be joyous about. Don't you?

Perhaps you've been in the trenches so long you've forgotten how to recognize joy. Joy is receiving a play check from a child who wrote out the draft to you just for being a nice mommy. Joy is the son who adoringly allows you to take a turn being Spider-Man because you make the "bestest webs." Joy is drinking hot cocoa in the kitchen after bedtime with the lights low and gazing at the face of your beloved. Joy is staying in your jammies for an extra hour on Saturday morning. Joy is the swell of your heart when it is overcome in worship. Joy is the sweet feel of your toddler's chubby hand in yours. Joy is hearing your baby's first cry after hours of hard labor. Joy is watching your child perform in his first school play. It is bright red polish on toes peeking out of summer sandals. It is watching the sheets on the line soaking up pungent sunshine smells and knowing you have a dryer for backup should the clouds come in. It is answered prayer. It is ephemeral now, but it will one day last for eternity.

During a rough patch, it's even possible to manufacture some joy. After all, right feelings often follow right actions. So *act* joyful, even if you don't feel it. Try these acts of joy:

+ *Play*. Chase. Old Maid. Go fish. Battleship. Twister. Hide 'n' seek. Dress up. Make a tent out of the table. Cover a flashlight with red tissue paper, secure it with a rubber band, and "camp" out.

+ *Savor*. The creamy flavor of ice cream and the crunch of the cone. The comforting smell of chocolate-chip-oatmeal cookies baking in the oven. The glossy slickness of a brand new magazine. The earthy smell after a rain. The cool feeling of silk. The sweet smell of a freshly bathed baby. The sound of tinkling drops of rain on the windowpane. The warm, strong touch of your husband's hand.

+ *Slow down*. Walk somewhere instead of driving. Deliberately slow your gait. Ride your bicycle. You really don't forget how! Pick wild flowers. Rake the leaves for the sole purpose of jumping in them.

+ *Smile*. Ever notice the incredible difference it makes when you motion a car to go ahead of you in heavy traffic and you do it with a smile? Or when you shrug your shoulders and grin like an idiot when you've made a dumb driving error? When you stand in line at the grocery store and upon noticing the poor soul behind you has only a loaf of bread and a gallon of milk and you smile and say, "Go ahead of me. I'm not in a hurry." Smiling is contagious. It makes friends. It disarms enemies.

+ *Serve*. Bake cookies for the widow living in a retirement home. Decorate the outside of an envelope containing a cheery note of encouragement, a card for a college student, a soldier serving far away. Surprise your family by cheerfully waiting on them as they dine from TV trays during your favorite Christmas classic movie.

Choosing Joy

The essence of joy isn't really that elusive. It's just that with adulthood, along with the privilege of eating your pie before your broccoli, come the dubious honors of bill paying, floor scrubbing, and knowing that there is evil lurking as close as the evening news. We find ourselves anticipating the worst. Getting mired in the muck of daily cares. Jesus wisely cautioned us not to borrow trouble by worrying. It steals joy, and "each day has enough trouble of its own" (Matthew 6:34).

We can shape each day with our choices. In the movie *Open Range*, Kevin Costner's character, Charlie, said of Mose, "He was the kind of man who'd say 'Good morning!' and mean it, whether it was or not." Wouldn't it be nice if that could be said of us, regardless of sleepless nights walking a colicky baby, or days spent mopping vomit just inches from the trashcan or toilet? Even on the days when we're housebound with a killer case of cabin fever!

How long has it been since you've walked in the rain? Splashed in the puddles? Seen animal shapes in the clouds? Gotten a sundae with extra hot fudge and not thought once about the calories? Sung along with the radio, not caring how you sounded? Try it, and see if joy breaks out.

Just for today, live in a fairy tale. Act like your home is a castle. Dress like a princess. Laugh more. Lie down against the contrast of a satin pillowcase and flannel sheets. Smile every chance you get. Recapture the magic of "let's pretend." Dust off your dreams. Life is good. Joyful, even. It's just that in the flurry of living it, we've forgotten.

Some day all too soon, there will come a last. A last tucking in. A last request to "come wipe me." A last car seat. A last booster. A last meal in the high chair. A last late-night hunt for that special pink sleepy bear. A last call for assistance tying shoes. A last spontaneous hug around your knees. A last night in the cradle, crib, or toddler bed. A last dusting of trophies, medals, field day ribbons, and Super Kid stickers. A last morning of fighting over who gets the toy in the cereal box. A last call of "Mom, can I borrow the car?" A last minute rush to find a shoe box or empty oatmeal container for those blasted dioramas. A last school program, concert, or game to attend.

Baby shoes will be traded for roller skates. Tricycles for ten-speeds. Bikes for cars with insurance. Pastel baby walls for endless posters and loud music. School rompers for athletic uniforms. Size 2T for size 14. Tooth fairies for braces. My eyes grow blurry with tears as I type. I don't so much want to have another baby but I long to freeze these days—to capture them and wring out every drop of sweetness before they are gone. Before the children fly the nest.

And they will. It's my job. It's the way God designed families to work. A difficult birth. A soft place to land. A high perch from which to spread wings and soar! And always, a place to which they can return for brief periods; from which they can hold your hand and beg you to come see what they've done with their own nests. Life goes on.

So tonight as you traipse wearily down the hall or up the stairs, crunching Barbie shoes, Hot Wheels, and Tinkertoys underfoot, rejoice. Because one day soon they'll be perched on a garage shelf awaiting the next rummage sale. Because one day soon, before you know it, you'll wish for a carousel centerpiece made of wooden disks and plastic rods to grace your table just one more time.

QUESTIONS FOR STUDY AND REFLECTION

1. Look up the following verses and answer the accompanying questions.

   James 4:14—To what does James compare our life? _____ This is why we are not to _____ _____ or to boast about tomorrow.

Psalm 39:4—"Show me my life's _____ and the _____ of my _____; let me know how _____ is my life."

Psalm 89:47—In this verse, David turns the tables and asks *God* to remember what? _____ Why do you think David does this?

Psalm 144:4—In a similar vein, David writes that a man is like a _____ and his days are like a fleeting _____.

2. Do verses like those depress you or motivate you to make the most of those days which you're given?

3. In Ecclesiastes, an Eeyorish King Solomon says that "death is the destiny of every man; the living should take this to heart" (7:2). How should such knowledge lend urgency to our parenting? Our friendships? Our relationship with our mate? With our Creator?

4. Ecclesiastes 5:19 lists five things that are gifts from God. Write them here:

   1.
   2.
   3.
   4.
   5.

   Have you ever thought that God can make you happy in your work no matter what it is? Why or why not?

5. Read Revelation 21:4. What a verse of hope for our future! Who is it that will be wiping our tears? _____ Himself. Ponder that awesome thought. If we lead our children to Him, then it will be worth it all when we stand before Jesus together—forever!

6. Do you feel affirmed in your decision to concentrate your best efforts

on homemaking? Why or why not? What difference would/does having a support system make? Do you fully realize God notices and approves your efforts?

7. If you knew that from today you only had one year left to impart your faith, values, and traditions to your children and to make memories with them, how would you live differently? Why not start today?

Action Plan

Determine that you will live each day more purposefully and seek God's assistance with this. Remember that nothing of value can be accomplished without His help. Ask for His help to exercise your faith, your hope, your love, your patience, and your joy. There is not a better tool kit with which to equip yourself for a fulfilled and radiant life as a wife and mother. I will be praying for you as you complete your journey.

Journal

Write a narrative description of your best memory as a child. Dig deep and haul out a stunning memory from your childhood archives. Share the story with your children sometime this week.

Remember to jot down those precious phrases and little happenings that make up daily life. It will be a gift to yourself and your children which you can treasure together.

Memorize

"Show me, O Lord, my life's end and the number of my days; let me know how fleeting is my life" (Psalm 39:4).

Tools and Tricks of the Trade

Greeting-Card Box

One helpful tool for organization is a greeting-card box with monthly dividers. Write down all birthdays and anniversaries on each divider. At the beginning of each month, check to see what types of cards you need, then purchase or make them all at once. Children love using rubber stamp sets to create their own cards. Check out discount card and party outlets or order cards in bulk from places like Current. Other companies, like Guideposts, have encouragement card clubs, which send you a variety pack each month. Whenever you find that perfect birthday card or laugh-out-loud encouragement card, you can purchase it and file it away in a spot where you can actually find it again. Keep wedding, sympathy, and get-well cards on hand. A supply of general birthday cards, thank-you notes, and blank cards can see you through nearly every occasion without any last-minute shopping.

I also include a special section in my box of romantic or funny cards to send to Greg, and another section just for silly or encouraging cards to remind my girlfriends they are precious to me even when our schedules aren't allowing for much talk time.

Always buy Christmas cards at the after-Christmas sales. If you're really ambitious, you could make homemade cards with stickers and stamps by doing just a few each month. If you like to send a family picture as your card, keep an eye out every time you develop a roll of film for that perfect snapshot—it's usually much less expensive than a studio-made card.

Warranty/Manual Organizer with Pockets

Are you forever looking for the receipt to prove when a broken appliance was purchased? Wondering where that manual is when the bread machine won't reset? Have no idea how to clean the supposedly self-cleaning oven? Current and Colorific catalogs and many office-supply stores all sell these. When you purchase any major appliance, lawn and garden aid, furniture, or smaller appliances like clock radios, phones, or microwaves, staple the receipt to the front of the manual, write the date purchased on the manual, and highlight the date and type of appliance.

Bill-Paying System

After ten years of trial and error experimentation with the best way to organize and pay bills, my favorite method uses three items: bill-paying folders, a spiral notebook, and a wooden 31-day organizer with slots. Office-supply stores and many catalogs sell both bill-paying folders and the wooden organizers. I have even seen one of the wooden organizers at Target recently.

Here's how I organize our bills. As soon as a bill comes in the mail, I immediately open it, review the statement for errors, file it if necessary, and then tuck the return portion of the bill under the flap of the envelope and place it in the allotted compartment of the bill-paying organizer. You may label individual pocket folders for mortgage, car payment, phone bills, credit cards, school loans, household expenses, taxes, entertainment, and so on.

Our payday is once at the end of the month. That evening I sit down with the organizer, the checkbook, and the spiral notebook. I use one page of the notebook for every month. At the top, I write down our first "bills"— our tithe (read Exodus 23:19). In keeping with that principle, I list the places to which we give as a reminder that our firstfruits go to God. Most of our tithe goes to our local church. But we also support several other ministries, including my sister and her family, who serve as missionaries in Taiwan. If God has blessed us with extra, some months we may give to various other worthy charities as well. Remember, though, it isn't possible to support every cause, or your allotted dollars will be stretched too far to do much good.

Where you choose to give is a private matter—however, I encourage you to practice giving back to God what is His in the first place. Although it is tempting to skip tithing while on a tight one-income budget, giving sets a profound example for your children. I have seen God provide for my family and heard many other stories of His care for His children.

In the spiral notebook I enter every bill and the amount. This ensures that I don't forget anything. I used to be notorious about forgetting the automatic withdrawal payments. And it provides me with an easy way to figure average bill amounts for electric, water, and so on. I place a colored checkmark next to each item after I have written the check. Here's a sample notebook entry:

September Checks	
Tithe:	Villa Heights Christian Church
	Ozark Christian College
	Life Choices
	Team Expansion—Taiwan
	Focus on the Family
	Children's Center of S.W. Missouri
Mortgage	

September Checks	
Electric	
Water/sewage/trash	
Van payment	
Phone	
Cell phone	
Car/life/house insurance	
Health insurance	
Graduate-school loan	
Gymnastics lessons (Emmy and Ellie)	
Visa	
Groceries	
Gas	
Stamps	
Dry-cleaning	
Savings	
Retirement	
Medical bills	

After the checks for the bills are all written out, and before I seal them in their envelopes, I write the date each bill needs to be mailed on the corner where the stamp goes. Then I file them in the corresponding slot in the wooden slotted organizer. For example, if I have a bill that needs to reach JC Penney on the fifteenth of the month, then I put it in the eleventh day slot. This helps me stay organized, and since bills are gradually going out over the course of the month, more of my money stays with me, providing a small interest-bearing cushion. While you're at it, go through your greeting-card box and place each card in the slot with the date they need to be mailed. Everyone will be so impressed that you can remember their birthdays and anniversaries!

Of course, many people are now choosing to use check cards and online bill-paying services. However, I still prefer to keep a paper trail in front of me. If you're disciplined enough, you could try this—one family I know puts everything from groceries to hardware bills on their Visa, and then they simply write one check at month's end. The choice is individual and should reflect what is easiest and makes the most sense for your lifestyle.

Message Center with a Family Calendar

Above our phone table we have a small wood-framed magnetic board that doubles as a dry-erase board. We can post invitations and reminders with the magnets, as well as leave messages or begin lists. At the bottom are two hooks that serve as the permanent place for us to put our keys, saving us from the usual morning game of "Let's find the car keys!" Next to the phone, I have a small notepad, which I change every month, much to my girls' delight. They love being able to borrow a sheet, take a message, or receive a note on anything from a barn to a snowman to a heart or ladybug! We also have an oversized, colorful laminated bookmark that has our phone number, address, our names, and the large letters 9-1-1 listed to help flustered young ones remember what to do in case of an emergency.

On the wall nearby is our family calendar that lists *all* family member's events. I highly recommend keeping your version by the phone and having a family calendar in addition to your own personal calendar on which to record, in more detail, tasks or reminders.

Gift Box

I don't know that this idea is original with me—I have always had one—but everywhere I go, women are always asking me to "slow down so we can write this down!" So here I am, writing it down for you! I have a *gigantic* clear plastic box with a lid that I keep in a craft/ironing board/miscellaneous closet downstairs. As I find things I know will be perfect for someone's birthday or other occasion (a gift for my secret pal in our women's ministry program; the perfect stocking stuffer—in April), it goes in the box. I also store baby gifts (calendars, journals, frames, small-size boy or girl infant outfits as I find them on sale), photo albums, stationery, candles, coloring books, crayons, Barbies, earrings, lotion, CDs, ornaments, trinkets for Valentine's Day and Easter baskets, colorful notepads, and various baskets.

Whenever I put something into the gift box, I jot it down on a paper log. When the gift is given, I mark a line through it. That way I don't have to dig all the way through the box wondering if I have any picture frames left. I also make a special notation if I purchased something for someone specific. For example, American Girl sewing notecards—Emmy—Easter basket. This enables me to shop thoughtfully and within my budget. I can store gifts efficiently and never get caught without a gift for a colleague, friend, unexpected special occasion—or a child's birthday party, when one of my girls announces to me with great nonchalance that they'd like to go to a classmate's party beginning in, oh, 30 minutes!

Gift-Wrap Center

If at all possible, create your gift-wrap center near your gift box. Jill Savage, founder of Hearts at Home, uses an old chest of drawers as her gift wrap center (I'm jealous!). I have a long rectangular gift wrap storage box (Rubbermaid) which hold 15 rolls of gift wrap, including jumbo rolls, and comes with two trays for storing tissue paper, bows, ribbon, raffia, gift tags, and gift sacks. If you have an extra pair, keeping scissors and tape in the box is also a great idea. If space is an issue, Current and Lillian Vernon both make cloth gift wrap organizers with Velcro tabs to hold wrapping paper rolls and clear inside pockets for holding flat gift wrap, sacks, and bows. They fit under the bed nicely.

Menu Planning and Family-Friendly Recipes

Quick School-Morning Breakfast Ideas

+ Lay out cereal in bowls with spoons and vitamins the night before.
+ Make one day a week a Pop-Tart or toaster-pastry morning and serve them on inexpensive paper doilies.
+ Make a batch of this wonderful honey-bran muffin mix and store in an airtight container in the fridge for fresh-from-the-oven muffins even during the week. One of these and an apple makes a great breakfast on the run should you ever oversleep.

Honey-Bran Muffins

1 15-ounce box bran flake cereal

1 cup vegetable oil

2 ½ cups sugar

4 eggs

5 teaspoons cinnamon

1 quart buttermilk

5 cups flour

5 teaspoons baking soda

2 teaspoons salt

Mix dry ingredients. Add butter, milk, oil, and eggs. Mix well.

Store in refrigerator for up to four weeks.

Bake in muffin tins (liners are much less messy on hectic mornings) at 400° for 18 minutes.

Blueberry-Oatmeal Breakfast Cake

1⅓ cups all-purpose flour

¾ cup quick rolled oats

⅓ cup sugar

2 teaspoons baking powder

¼ teaspoon salt

1 egg

¾ cup milk

¼ cup oil

1 cup frozen blueberries

Combine dry ingredients, then other ingredients in small bowls. Mix and add all at once to dry mixture. Spread in round baking dish. Bake 20 minutes at 400°.

Drizzle warm cake with powdered sugar icing (½ cup powdered sugar to 2 to 4 teaspoons milk).

Healthy Fast Food

Here are some great, fast ideas for breakfast.

+ Wash and slice fresh fruit each week when you get back from shopping, store in separate containers in fridge, and toss with strawberry yogurt for an easy, pleasing fruit salad.

+ Instant packets of oatmeal; garnish with a dollop of butter and brown sugar.

+ Toaster waffles (store-bought—or make your own in advance and use freezer bags) can be topped with cream cheese and fruit or peanut butter on the go; yogurt and fruit at home is a change from the usual butter and syrup.

+ Small, plastic containers of plain Cheerios and half a banana are another great rushed-morning breakfast-to-go.

Enjoy these simple suggestions for lunches at home or for the lunch box:

+ Yogurt

+ String cheese

+ Packaged peanut butter and crackers or cheese and crackers

+ Fruit cups—wait for a sale, or make up your own each week using small Tupperware containers.

+ Soup—bean with bacon, goldfish noodle, chicken noodle, and alphabet vegetable are big hits with my kids.

+ Applesauce

+ Add a slice of ham to a grilled cheese sandwich. Drizzle sweet potato slices with olive oil and bake for healthier fries. Dust with kosher salt and serve with low-fat ranch dipping sauce.

+ Frozen fish sticks (the kind without fillers) and frozen mixed vegetables are good nutritious items to keep on hand for home lunches.

- Pocket bread filled with shredded deli meats, shredded cheese, cherry tomato slices, shredded lettuce, and topped with poppyseed dressing is delicious.

- Buy a sandwich sealer and make up a loaf's worth of PB&J sandwiches, put in freezer bags; they will thaw perfectly by lunchtime at school.

- Put thin slices of Colby Jack cheese in between two flour tortillas, microwave for 1½ to 2 minutes, cut into triangles, and serve with salsa, guacamole, or sour cream.

- Let kids make minisandwiches with cheese, meat, and crackers—or peanut butter and crackers—to create their own inexpensive version of Lunchables.

- Fill a Tupperware box with snack box items: graham crackers, fruit snacks, raisins, and occasionally the sugary sweet Hostess-type stuff.

- Make your own trail mix with dried banana chips, shelled sunflower seeds, dried apples, and M&M's.

- Drizzle apple slices with lemon juice to keep them from discoloring. Send with a small container of caramel ice cream topping mixed with peanut butter.

- Use cookie cutters to cut cheese or sandwiches into fun shapes.

Kid-Tested Recipes for the Martha-Impaired

My Friend Karen's Book Club Chicken Tortilla Soup

1 onion, chopped

2 14.5-ounce cans cream of mushroom soup

2 14.5-ounce cans cream of chicken soup

2 14.5-ounce cans chicken broth

2 cups milk

6 chicken breasts cooked, chopped

garlic salt to taste

½ packet chili seasoning

shredded Cheddar cheese

10-inch soft flour tortillas, torn in pieces

Mix all ingredients except cheese and tortillas. Put in large pot and cook on medium for 15 minutes and then simmer for 15 to 20 minutes more. Put shredded cheese and tortillas in bowls and also put on top of each bowl of soup before serving. Serve with a tossed green salad and colas.

My Friend Lori's Homemade "Olive Garden" Alfredo Sauce

½ 8-ounce package cream cheese

1 stick butter

2 cups heavy cream or half and half

dash of garlic

dash of basil

1 4- to 6-ounce bag of shredded Parmesan cheese

Heat cream cheese and butter on medium until melted. Add cream and spices. Add in Parmesan cheese. Stir slowly. Turn down heat and simmer on low for at least 45 minutes, to enhance flavor. Pour over frozen plain cheese tortellini shells or any kind of egg noodles. Also make bread sticks or garlic toast and let kids help pitch in by making fun vegetable people with carrots, celery, yellow peppers, lettuce, pretzel sticks, and peanut butter or ranch dressing for dipping to accompany this meal.

Spaghetti Pizza Deluxe

1 12-ounce package thin spaghetti, cooked and drained

½ cup milk

2 eggs

2 small cans tomato sauce

Crumbled ground beef (amount to your taste), cooked and browned with onion and green pepper

Italian seasonings

garlic salt

8 ounces (about 1 cup) shredded Mozzarella cheese

Toss spaghetti with milk and eggs and spread mixture in a 9 x 13 baking dish. Top with tomato sauce and ground beef mixture, add seasonings, and sprinkle cheese on top. Cover dish with foil and bake 25 minutes in a 325° oven. After cooling slightly, cut into squares.

Broccoli-Cheese Soup

2 14.5-ounce cans cream of mushroom soup

1 14.5-ounce can cream of celery soup

3 cups milk

⅓ to ½ large carton Velveeta cheese

1 10-ounce package frozen, chopped broccoli

⅓ chopped onion, sautéed in 1 tablespoon butter

Cut cheese into chunks. Mix all ingredients together. Cook on low, stirring occasionally, until smooth and warm. Approximately 1 hour. This can also be done in 4 to 5 hours on low in the Crock-Pot. Be sure to stir occasionally and add cheese only during the last 2 hours.

Sprinkle with oyster crackers and serve with homemade rolls, celery sticks filled with peanut butter, and icy drinks. This is easily doubled for company.

Baked Potato Bar

Bake several medium-size potatoes. (Peel skins for younger children.)

Allow kids to top their own potatoes as much as possible.

Topping suggestions:

> bacon bits, fried crisp and crumbled
>
> shredded Cheddar cheese
>
> butter
>
> sour cream
>
> canned, heated chili
>
> steamed broccoli
>
> chopped green onions

For variety, bake sweet potatoes instead. They're a great source of essential vitamins. Top with butter, cinnamon, brown sugar, and chopped pecans.

One-Step Macaroni and Cheese

> 2 cups uncooked elbow macaroni
>
> 3½ cups milk
>
> 1 teaspoon Worcestershire sauce
>
> ½ teaspoon salt
>
> 2½ cups shredded Cheddar cheese
>
> paprika

In greased 13 x 9 baking dish, stir uncooked macaroni, milk, Worcestershire sauce, salt, and 1½ cups cheese until well blended. Cover *tightly* with foil.

Bake in 350° oven for 50 minutes (no peeking).

Uncover; top with remaining 1 cup cheese and sprinkle with paprika

Bake 10 minutes more or until cheese is melted.

Let stand 10 minutes before serving. Makes 6-8 servings. My kids love this with fish sticks.

Easy Crock-Pot Barbeque Pulled Pork

1 large boneless pork loin roast

½ cup apple cider vinegar

½ cup Worcestershire sauce

2 tablespoons melted butter

2 tablespoons flour

1 cup boiling water

1 bottle Heinz chili sauce (or other brand)

1 tablespoon chili seasoning

2 tablespoons garlic salt

1 cup brown sugar

Top roast with all ingredients and cook in Crock-Pot on low heat for 8 to 10 hours. A half-hour before serving, add 1 bottle of barbeque sauce, your choice.

Serve on split sandwich rolls with baked chips, cherry tomatoes, carrots and dip.

Pasta con Broccoli

1 bunch fresh broccoli flowers

3 tablespoons olive oil

1-3 tablespoons minced garlic

1 teaspoon black pepper

2 ¼ cups water

8-ounce spaghetti

¼-pound (6 to 8) slices hard salami, cut in strips

1 cup Parmesan cheese

Sauté broccoli, garlic in oil in large skillet. Season with pepper. Stir in water and spaghetti. Cover with lid and bring to boil. Cook over medium heat, stirring occasionally for approximately 15 minutes until pasta is tender.

Stir in salami and cheese. Heat through.

Extra Special Hamburgers

Idea #1: Use seasoning pepper and kosher salt to season burgers. Top with baby Swiss cheese. Serve on buttered and lightly toasted English muffins.

Idea #2: Add 1 tablespoon sugar, 1 tablespoon soy sauce, 3 tablespoons toasted sesame seeds to 1 pound of hamburger. Grill as usual.

Idea #3: Top burgers with salsa and Pepper Jack cheese.

Seasoned Oyster Crackers

1 package Hidden Valley Ranch dry dressing mix

¾ cup salad oil

6 cups plain oyster crackers

¼ teaspoon garlic powder

¼ teaspoon dill weed

Combine spices with oil. Pour over crackers; stir to coat. Place in 250° oven for 15 to 20 minutes. Stir halfway through. Cool and store in airtight container.

Family Night/Superbowl Seven-Layer Mexican Dip

1 large can refried beans

1 package taco seasoning

Mix together and spread in bottom of oblong dish.

Layer in order:
    1 16-ounce carton avocado dip
    1 16-ounce carton low-fat sour cream
    1 4-ounce can chopped ripe olives
    1 4-ounce can chopped green chiles
    1 8-ounce package shredded Monterey Jack cheese

Refrigerate until ready to use. Serve with Fritos scoops or curved tortilla chips for dipping.

Summer Vegetable Pizza
    2 cans Crescent rolls

Press together on cookie sheet or pizza pan. Bake as directed—cool 30 minutes.

Mix together:
    8 ounces cream cheese
    1 small packet Hidden Valley Ranch dry salad dressing
    1 cup Miracle Whip

Spread on cooled Crescent crust.

Top with various raw vegetables and grated cheese:
    broccoli
    mushrooms
    tomatoes (half cherry or grape tomatoes work best)
    carrots
    cauliflower
    yellow and green peppers

Desserts and Snacks

Butterscotch Dumplings

¾ cup brown sugar

¼ cup light corn syrup

2 tablespoons butter

1 teaspoon vanilla

1 package refrigerated biscuits

sour cream

In medium saucepan combine brown sugar, butter, and vanilla. Cook and stir until bubbly. Place biscuits on top. Simmer 10 minutes; cover and simmer 10 minutes more. Serve warm in dessert dishes; spoon sauce over top. Top with sour cream for adults; ice cream for kids. We usually need to double this.

Easiest Homemade Ice Cream Ever

2 boxes instant French vanilla pudding

1 box instant chocolate fudge pudding

1 ½ cups sugar

2 12-ounce cans Milnot

1 ½ teaspoon vanilla

Mix in order given and pour into ice-cream freezer. Finish filling to the fill line with Milnot. Freeze with salt and ice in electric or hand crank freezer.

Peanut-Butter Silk Pie

Filling:

1 8-ounce package cream cheese, softened

1 cup sugar

1 cup creamy peanut butter
1 tablespoon melted butter
1 teaspoon vanilla
1 cup heavy cream, beaten until stiff

Crust:
1 9-inch chocolate cookie-crumb crust

Topping:
1 cup semisweet chocolate chips
2 tablespoons coffee
chopped peanuts for garnish

Make filling: Beat cream cheese, sugar, peanut butter, butter, and vanilla in large mixing bowl until creamy. Gently fold in half of beaten cream and then fold in remaining cream until blended. Spread into crust; smooth top.

Make topping: Combine chocolate chips and coffee in microwave-proof bowl. Cover with plastic wrap. Microwave on high 2 minutes until smooth. Cool chocolate slightly, then pour over top of filling.

Refrigerate pie 1 hour until chocolate is firm. Sprinkle with chopped peanuts. For easier serving, chill overnight. Makes 8 servings.

Christmas Mix

1 pound white-chocolate bark
6 cups Crispix
3 cups Cheerios
1 pound bag of red & green M&M's
2 cups mixed nuts
2-3 cups small pretzels

Melt white-chocolate bark in microwave, stirring every 1 to 2 minutes until smooth. Toss with dry ingredients in large bowl. Let set. Turn out on waxed paper and break apart.

This mix looks extremely festive and elegant.

Daily Planner

Day _____ Date _____

8:00 _____

9:00 _____

10:00 _____

11:00 _____

12:00 _____

1:00 _____

2:00 _____

3:00 _____

4:00 _____

5:00 _____

6:00 _____

Evening: _____

_____

_____

God:	
Husband:	
Self:	
Children:	
Growth:	

Daily Planner

Day _____. Date _____

8:00 _____

9:00 _____

10:00 _____

11:00 _____

12:00 _____

1:00 _____

2:00 _____

3:00 _____

4:00 _____

5:00 _____

6:00 _____

Evening: _____

_____

_____

God:	
Husband:	
Self:	
Children:	
Growth:	

Daily Planner

Day _____ Date _____

8:00 _____

9:00 _____

10:00 _____

11:00 _____

12:00 _____

1:00 _____

2:00 _____

3:00 _____

4:00 _____

5:00 _____

6:00 _____

Evening: _____

_____

_____

God:	
Husband:	
Self:	
Children:	
Growth:	

Daily Planner

Day _____ Date _____

8:00 _____

9:00 _____

10:00 _____

11:00 _____

12:00 _____

1:00 _____

2:00 _____

3:00 _____

4:00 _____

5:00 _____

6:00 _____

Evening: _____

_____

_____

God:
Husband:
Self:
Children:
Growth:

Daily Planner

Day _____ Date _____

Time	
8:00	_____
9:00	_____
10:00	_____
11:00	_____
12:00	_____
1:00	_____
2:00	_____
3:00	_____
4:00	_____
5:00	_____
6:00	_____
Evening:	_____
	_____
	_____

God: _____

Husband: _____

Self: _____

Children: _____

Growth: _____

Daily Planner

Day _____ Date _____

8:00 _____

9:00 _____

10:00 _____

11:00 _____

12:00 _____

1:00 _____

2:00 _____

3:00 _____

4:00 _____

5:00 _____

6:00 _____

Evening: _____

_____

_____

God:	
Husband:	
Self:	
Children:	
Growth:	

Daily Planner

Day _____ Date _____

8:00 _____

9:00 _____

10:00 _____

11:00 _____

12:00 _____

1:00 _____

2:00 _____

3:00 _____

4:00 _____

5:00 _____

6:00 _____

Evening: _____

_____

_____

God:

Husband:

Self:

Children:

Growth:

Daily Planner

Day _____ Date _____

8:00 _____

9:00 _____

10:00 _____

11:00 _____

12:00 _____

1:00 _____

2:00 _____

3:00 _____

4:00 _____

5:00 _____

6:00 _____

Evening: _____

_____

_____

God: _____

Husband: _____

Self: _____

Children: _____

Growth: _____

Notes

Chapter 2

1. *Ladies' Home Journal*, March 2004, p. 51.
2. *Ladies' Home Journal*, March 2004, p. 52.
3. *Ladies' Home Journal*, March 2004, p. 53.
4. Ann Pleshette Murphy, *Family Circle*, October 19 2004, p. 53.
5. *Ladies' Home Journal*, May 2004, p. 30.
6. *Family Circle*, May 21, 2002, p. 62.
7. Tony Campolo, *You Can Make a Difference* (Nashville, TN: W Publishing Group, 2003), p. 51.
8. Early Stages, *Focus On Your Child*, June/July 2004, p. 8.

Chapter 9

1. *Ladies' Home Journal*, May 2004, p. 142.
2. *Ladies' Home Journal*, July 2004, p. 68.
3. *Parents*, May 2004, p. 54.
4. *Ladies' Home Journal*, October 2003, p. 179.
5. *Ladies' Home Journal*, July 2004, p. 58.

Chapter 12

1. *Ladies' Home Journal*, March 2003, p. 113.
2. Debra Evans, *Blessing Your Husband* (Wheaton, IL: Focus on the Family/Tyndale Publishers, 2003), p. 23.
3. Adapted from Cindy Sigler Dagnan, "Unfaithful Lessons," *The Lookout*, January 2003, p. 7.
4. *Today's Christian Woman*, January/February 2005, p. 28.

Chapter 13

1. *Family Circle*, November 17, 1998, p. 23.

About the Author

Cindy Sigler Dagnan has a passion for families: encouraging weary moms, cheering on desperate housewives, championing marriages in this age of disposable ones, making the most of the tender years in which God entrusts to us our little ones. She loves writing and speaking about those topics.

If you would like to have Cindy speak or would like to schedule a marriage seminar with Cindy and her husband, Greg, you may contact her through her website at **www.cindydagnan.com**. She always enjoys hearing from her readers.

MOTHERHOOD:
The Guilt That Keeps On Giving
Julie Ann Barnhill

Do you ever feel guilty for mistakes you've made as a mom—real and perceived? For not acting the way other people expect a mom to act? For not living up to your own expectations of mothering perfection?

You're not alone. Julie Barnhill has been there, and the hundreds of surveys she's collected reveal that many other moms feel the same way. With a good supply of humor and lots of understanding, Julie will gently guide you out of rugged Guiltmore National Park. On the way, you'll discover...

+ the difference between false (imagined) guilt and real guilt
+ the pitfalls of unrealistic expectations and overconfidence
+ God's path to less guilt and more grace

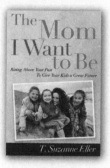

THE MOM I WANT TO BE
**Rising Above Your Past to Give
Your Kids a Great Future**
T. Suzanne Eller

Your experience as a mother—and a woman—is influenced by the mothering you received as a child. If neglect or inconsistency was a part of your upbringing, you need a healthy vision of the wonderful thing motherhood can be.

Suzie Eller gently, compassionately gives you a godly, nurturing model. From her own difficult experience, she reveals how bitterness and anger can be transformed into hope. She walks beside you and shows you...

+ how shattered legacies can be put back together
+ ways to forgive, let go, and leave your parenting baggage in the past
+ how to give your kids the gift of good memories and a great future

"Offers tangible help so we can pass on the best of who we are to our children and grandchildren... Thanks, Suzie, for handing moms a tool chest full of help and hope!"

Pam Farrel
coauthor of *Got Teens?* and *Men Are Like Waffles, Women Are Like Spaghetti*

Red-hot Monogamy
Making Your Marriage Sizzle
Bill and Pam Farrel

Did you know that the best sexual experiences are enjoyed by married couples? Marriage and relationship experts Bill and Pam Farrel reveal what you need to know to add spark and sizzle to your love life. You'll discover how

+ God specifically designed you to give and receive pleasure from your mate
+ a little skill turns marriage into red-hot monogamy
+ sex works best emotionally, physically, and physiologically

Along with ways to create intimacy when you're just too tired and how to avoid the "pleasure thieves," this book offers hundreds more ideas to inspire romance and passion in every aspect of your lives together.

Romancing Your Husband
Enjoying a Passionate Life Together
Debra White Smith

Debra reveals how you can create a union others only dream about. From making Jesus an active part of your marriage to arranging fantastic romantic interludes, you'll discover how to "knock your husband's socks off"; become a *lover-wife*, not a *mother-wife*; and ultimately, cultivate a sacred romance with God.

Experience fulfillment through romancing your husband...and don't be surprised when he romances you back!

If Mama Ain't Happy, Ain't Nobody Happy
Making the Choice to Rejoice
Lindsey O'Connor

Could you use some sparkle in your life? In this bestselling resource, Lindsey O'Connor shares encouraging, everyday-life examples and stories and uncovers the hidden struggles women meet on their way to joy. Realistic but affirming, this veteran mom and author helps you find...

+ balance in the process
+ new meaning in daily tasks
+ contentment where you are

There really is joy to be found in the mom experience—it's God's joy. And that's something that makes life worth celebrating!